WHAT OTHERS ARE SAYING

The voices that follow come from people who have seen this work unfold—in conference rooms, through seasons of change, and at moments when clarity mattered most. Some walked alongside me as colleagues and mentors. Others entrusted me with their life's work and legacy.

The individual person(s) (promoters) listed below have not been paid/compensated, directly or indirectly, for their comments/opinions (testimonials or endorsements). That the testimonial was given by a current client or investor, and the endorsement was given by a person other than a current client or investor, as applicable. That cash or non-cash compensation was not provided for the testimonial or endorsement. THE IMPACT PARTNERSHIP, LLC is an Insurance Marketing Organization that helps promote the advertising and marketing activities of the firm. Therefore, there may be material conflicts of interest on the part of the person giving the testimonial or endorsement resulting from the firm's relationship with such person related to THE IMPACT PARTNERSHIP, LLC.

I love the title of this book. Read it. It explains Jackie perfectly. Most financial planners help clients with their money. My experience with Jackie showed that it wasn't just about the money, for the client or for her. It was, and has always been, about the personal joy we experience when we help someone else succeed, in retirement or otherwise. Read the book. As a financial planner and an attorney who practices in the tax arena, helping practices like Jackie's with strategic growth, it was such an incredible experience to see a CPA and financial advisor who actually knew and cared about creating a roadmap for her clients. It was watching the smile on her face when her clients recognized that they were living the life they envisioned. To watch her lead her team in creating solutions to not only income planning but also ensuring, to the extent possible, that they always paid the least amount of taxes legally possible, their estate was situated, and removing the fear of growing old, it was inspiring. For her to take that knowledge, drive, and passion and share it in her newest book is what I would consider an incredible gift that should not be passed up. Her passion is about helping you find your passion in retirement. Read the book!

—**Michael Canet,** JD, LLM
Managing Director & Founder
Prostatis Group, LLC DBA:
Prostatis Financial Advisors Group
A non-client of the firm. No compensation was paid for this endorsement.

This book is a must-read for anyone serious about their finances and retirement. As an industry friend, it's very clear to see that Jackie has a genuine desire to help people through sound financial education and planning. This book helps to simplify financial planning and will give you actionable steps you can take right away to help improve your financial plan. I highly recommend Jackie and this book, *Beyond the Money*, as it will be a valuable resource for years to come.

—**Abe Abich**, Founder and CEO
Abich Financial Services, Inc.
A non-client of the firm. No compensation was paid for this endorsement.

When I retired from the Army 25 years ago, we moved to a new job location, and we needed to file three state tax returns and our federal return. Hiring Campbell & Company to help with our tax returns began a meaningful relationship of professional support and learning about tax savings and smarter investments for many more years. Our savings are now focused on retention and protection for future retirement needs. We totally trust the advice received from Jackie Campbell, and that is why we brought our granddaughters and daughter-in-law to her firm to help them, too.

—**David Gust**, Major General
US Army Retired
Client of the firm. Testimonial was given by this current client, but no compensation was paid for this testimonial.

Choosing a financial advisor is fundamentally about trust, and in all my years of working with top-tier advisors, Jackie Campbell stands out as someone who blends immense expertise with an unmatched dedication to people. She turns retirement planning into something deeply personal, focusing not just on financial security, but on embracing life's best moments with confidence and confetti. By blending decades of experience with a sincere dedication to joy, family, and legacy, Jackie truly goes "beyond the money." What makes her exceptional is how she embodies both top-level credentials (CFP, CPA, PFS) and a genuine warmth that makes her more than just an advisor. She's a trusted partner in building a legacy of love and memories for future generations. Simply put, she treats you like family while making sure your retirement dreams are secure. And because of all this, trusting Jackie isn't just a choice–it's a natural conclusion. She simply can't help but earn that trust, making her the foundation of a confident and joyful retirement journey.

—**Ron Eastman**, Sr. VP of Advisor Growth
THE IMPACT PARTNERSHIP, LLC
A non-client of the firm. No compensation was paid for this endorsement.

In my thirty years of interacting with Jackie Campbell's firm, either by tax consultation and filings or wealth management and investments, my wife and I have always felt we've been blessed with the best company qualified to lead us into our retirement years.

—**John & Sue Edwards**
Client of the firm. Testimonial was given by this current client, but no compensation was paid for this testimonial.

Jackie's approach combines decades of expertise with a genuine commitment to helping people retire with clarity and confidence. *Beyond the Money* reflects the same thoughtful guidance I've experienced working with her—practical, insightful, and focused on what truly matters.

—**Kim Skouras**, Chief of Staff
THE IMPACT PARTNERSHIP, LLC
Client of the firm. Testimonial was given by this current client, but no compensation was paid for this testimonial

Working with Jackie Campbell has been a true professional highlight. She is insightful, thoughtful, and brings a steady confidence to everything she does. Co-hosting the *Beyond the Money* radio show and podcast alongside Jackie has been both incredibly rewarding. Her guiding principle, "Prior Planning Pays," is more than a motto; it reflects the disciplined, client-focused approach she brings to every conversation and relationship. I am both proud and grateful to call Jackie a colleague and a friend.

—**Mark Owens**, Radio Host
THE IMPACT PARTNERSHIP, LLC
Client of the firm. Testimonial was given by this current client, but no compensation was paid for this testimonial.

My sincere gratitude for Jackie and her staff for always helping me to make the right choices with my investments and taxes. I would have been totally lost after the death of my husband if not for Jackie. When I am gone, my children will benefit from this knowledge.

Love, **Anne Pallot**
Client of the firm. Testimonial was given by this current client, but no compensation was paid for this testimonial.

When I came to Jackie for my investment and retirement planning, I immediately knew I had found someone I could trust and who would act in my best interest. I feel completely confident in my retirement knowing that Jackie will assist me in planning what is best for me.

—**Davina Kidwell**
Client of the firm. Testimonial was given by this current client, but no compensation was paid for this testimonial.

BEYOND THE MONEY

THE ROADMAP TO RETIRING ON YOUR OWN TERMS WITH CLARITY, CONFIDENCE, AND DIRECTION

Beyond the Money

The Roadmap to Retiring on Your Own Terms with Clarity, Confidence, and Direction

Stop Procrastinating, Feel Prepared, and Cue the Confetti

Jackie Campbell

ethos collective

Printed in the United States of America

Published by Igniting Souls
PO Box 43, Powell, OH 43065
IgnitingSouls.com

LCCN: 2025919928
Paperback ISBN: 978-1-63680-571-9
Hardback ISBN: 978-1-63680-572-6
eBook ISBN: 978-1-63680-573-3

Available in paperback, hardcover, e-book, and audiobook.

Important Notice

This book is intended for educational and informational purposes only and is not intended to be used as marketing or sales material by financial professionals. It is not intended to provide tax, legal, investment, or financial advice specific to your situation. Financial decisions involve many variables, and laws and regulations change over time.

Before making decisions that may affect your finances, taxes, investments, insurance, or estate planning, you should consult with qualified professionals who can consider your individual circumstances. Reading this book does not create an advisor-client relationship.

Any examples shared are intended to illustrate planning concepts, not to recommend specific strategies or outcomes.

The superscript symbol IP listed throughout this book is known as the unique certification mark created and owned by Instant IP^{IP}. Its use signifies that the corresponding expression (words, phrases, chart, graph, etc.) has been protected by Instant IP^{IP} via smart contract. Instant IP^{IP} is designed with the patented smart contract solution (US Patent: 11,928,748), which creates an immutable time-stamped first layer and fast layer identifying the moment in time an idea is filed on the blockchain. This solution can be used in defending intellectual property protection. Infringing upon the respective intellectual property, i.e., IP, is subject to and punishable in a court of law.

Dedicated to

My Mother,
who taught me the value of faith,
family, and community and what it means to live with
grace, independence, and a caregiver's heart.
Your quiet strength shaped everything I am.

Scott,
my high school sweetheart, a Florida State Trooper,
and the best dad I know.
Thank you for providing unwavering protection,
clarity, and context as we built a life and
legacy together—personally and professionally.

My family—Brooke, Jacob, Chuck, Drew, and Stevie Bleu,
whose love, laughter, and presence
are my greatest confetti moments.
You are the reason behind the "why,"
and the legacy that
inspires every chapter—past, present, and still to come.

Contents

Part IV: Living Beyond the Money

A Note to the Reader

Retirement is not a financial event. I would like to think that it is a responsibility shift—from accumulation to stewardship, from urgency to order, and from proving to protecting.

I think everyone my age eventually says, "If I'd known then what I know now..." I heard it from my parents' generation. Thirty years later, I catch myself saying it too.

When you're twenty, you assume sixty is a distant concept—if you ever get there at all. And if you do, you imagine that somehow, magically, everything will already be figured out.

Some of us spend decades focused on work, savings, and responsibility. We worry about how much to save, how long to work, and whether retirement will arrive before our energy runs out.

But life is not a finish line. And when we plan as if it is, we miss the road in between.

I'm a Certified Financial Planner®, so I know better than most that we can't just sit on our hands or party for fifty years and hope Social Security lasts long enough to support us. But the majority of the people I serve live with a work, work, work mentality. They spend their entire lives saving for a rainy day. I'm hoping I can help a few see that there's a road to travel in between.

After working with retirees since graduation, I thought I

knew what hitting sixty would look like, but now that I'm here, I see it completely differently.

Enjoy Friends

Thirty years after their first big hit, Kenny Rogers and Dolly Parton recorded a song that resonates loudly now that I'm getting closer to retirement age. "You Can't Make Old Friends" holds so much truth, especially for the person hurrying through life with the intention of taking time for the most important things after they retire.

In the music video, Kenny Rogers says, "In this business, where so much of it is business, to take the time for a moment and just enjoy someone for the person they are is a great gift, and I appreciate you [Dolly] always doing that with me . . . and in this business, she is my best friend."[1]

When I hear that song, I start to think about the people who influenced me and helped me get where I am now. You can meet new friends every day, but you can't replace those relationships you forged in your youth or the early days of your business. One of my business partners has been part of this journey for over twenty-five years. We have many memories and much hard-won wisdom from our journey together. Then, as new people join our team, they bring fresh perspectives and energy that build on what already exists. They may not share the same history, but they become part of the story going forward. Experience provides the foundation; collaboration carries it forward.

My husband was a first responder, and I appreciate the tremendous camaraderie, tightness, and unity you see among law enforcement and the military. They have a cohesiveness that is invaluable.

I grew up on a small farm in a quaint community, and at

the time, I know I took for granted the close-knit ties that kind of upbringing created. I learned that when you see a neighbor in need, you help him. In a farming community, it's never each man for himself. And the closer I get to retirement and listen to the stories, I feel bad for the people I see who never take time to forge those friendships.

It's never too early to become intentional with the people who have impacted your life. I enjoy spending time with each one, and I try to let them know just how much I appreciate the contribution they made to my life—my mom, my husband, my children, grandchildren, and even my childhood friends who were my bridesmaids so many years ago.

IT'S NEVER TOO EARLY TO BECOME INTENTIONAL WITH THE PEOPLE WHO HAVE IMPACTED YOUR LIFE.

Pausing to spend time with old friends should be at the top of our list of things to do as we journey through life, even when you're in your twenties. Work will wait, but you never know when you will spend your last moment with those you admire, respect, and love.

Take Care of Yourself

That drive to increase your retirement payout often increases the closer you get to the date, but too few think about whether the lifestyle they're forcing on themselves while they build their 401(k) will let them enjoy the funds they're saving. What if I told you the quality of your health when you retire is more important than the quality of your investments?

When I started in this business, like some young people, I saw many who let stress steal their best years, or lost mobility early because they didn't take care of themselves. Still, I never thought anything like that could happen to me.

Even when you do your best, health concerns can interrupt your plans. I've learned this too well. But when you don't take care of yourself, it's inevitable. And you can't get back the health you worked away when you were young.

I've spent over thirty-three years in my own business. Working with entrepreneurs, business leaders, and hard-working everyday people has given me some insight into the things that bring success or create stumbling blocks for our retirement years. I've witnessed the outcomes of good planning, and I've seen the consequences of failing to plan.

No one can tell you exactly how to retire successfully because success depends on your goals, your values, and the life you want to live. However, I've discovered that some people aren't clear on what matters most to them, and without that clarity, even the best plan falls short.

I love helping people get clear on the legacy they want to leave and the choices that shape the road toward that legacy. That's why I've set out to create a roadmap that has the ability to transform uncertainty into Clarity, Direction, and Confidence in retirement. I want you to be intentional every step along the way so you can own your financial story and carry it Beyond the Money.

Over more than three decades, I've watched thousands of families arrive at the same moment—responsible, prepared, and still uncertain. I've seen what works, what fails quietly, and what creates regret years later. This book exists not as theory, but as distilled experience—built from outcomes, not opinions.

Part I: Understanding Your One Financial Life[IP] – Clarity

Where You Are

Before you can make confident financial decisions, you need to understand your One Financial Life—where you are today and how all the pieces fit together.

1

YOUR FINANCIAL STORY DIDN'T START WITH YOU

Though no one can go back and make a brand new start, anyone can start from now and make a brand new ending.
—Carl Bard

Forget the former things, do not dwell on the past.
—Isaiah 43:18

After more than thirty-three years of real-life outcomes, I've seen what works, what doesn't, and how financial decisions ripple through the lives of the ones they love most.

Not every retiree walks in with a pension, a business to sell, or wealth built through strategy. But everyone comes with a story.

Long before we make our first financial decision, we inherit beliefs about money. They form quietly, often without permission, long before we understand interest rates, retirement accounts, or tax brackets. It comes from the households we grew up in, the conversations we overheard, the worries we sensed, and the habits we watched modeled day after day.

Some learned to guard money. It seemed scarce. Other families never discussed the subject, but the children still saw it as plentiful. Many learned financial responsibility before confidence, discipline before ease, and some learned—without ever hearing it said out loud—that no matter how hard you work, it might still not be enough.

Not Quite Enough

I grew up in a home that clipped coupons and stretched every penny. I learned to pay attention to prices, waste nothing, and plan ahead because surprises were rarely good. Farm life, even on a small farm, teaches things that follow you for life. For instance, nothing grows without effort, timing matters, and weather, markets, and circumstances don't always cooperate, no matter how hard you work. And with these lessons comes humility.

That upbringing built discipline, gratitude, and resilience. It shaped my work ethic and my respect for preparation. Much of how I approach money, work, and planning today traces back to what I learned simply by watching my mother live out her values. But those same lessons also planted a belief that many capable, dependable people carry quietly into adulthood: more is never quite enough.

Sadly, that belief doesn't disappear just because your income increases. In fact, it often becomes louder.

I've worked with people who have done everything "right." They worked hard. They saved diligently and avoided foolish mistakes. They raised families, built businesses, and showed up consistently for decades. On paper, they look successful by almost any measure. And yet, when the decisions become bigger—retirement, business transitions, legacy planning—they don't feel confident.

Some are like Linda Roberts.

The Typical Retiree's Story

Linda worked for a mid-sized insurance firm for nearly thirty-five years. She started as a receptionist, moved to customer service, and eventually became an office manager.

Linda never cleared six figures, chased promotions, or worried about being wealthy. But they loved her at work. She was steady, faithful, disciplined, and proud of the life she'd built. Her familiar story isn't glamorous; however, it's exactly the kind of story the majority of retirees live.

When she came into my office at age sixty-six, she brought a folder with her printed account statements, Social Security estimates, Medicare notes, beneficiary designations, and a small pension from her very first job. She tapped the folder and whispered, "I hope this is enough. I really tried."

Maybe you feel like Linda. You've lived responsibly, but you still feel uneasy. Some retirees come to me with fear, but it's not a fear of spending; it's a fear of failing. They worry they've failed their children, their kids, themselves. Usually, those thoughts come from a financial story learned in the past—a story that no longer matches the season they're entering.

People who feel the most uncertain are often the most responsible—the planners and caretakers. To me, Linda feared becoming a burden. I felt like she was feeling powerless and afraid of making a mistake; she didn't make a move. In my opinion, lack of clarity left her paralyzed.

Clarity, Direction, Confidence

Many people don't need strategies or solutions; I believe they need Clarity, Direction, and Confidence. These three anchors describe the internal experience each of us needs to navigate living Beyond the Money.

PEOPLE DON'T NEED STRATEGIES OR SOLUTIONS; I BELIEVE THEY NEED CLARITY, DIRECTION, AND CONFIDENCE.

I think of financial planning like driving. Before I get in the car, I need clarity about where I'm going. I don't need every detail of the trip, but I do need to know the destination and why it matters. Without that, every mile feels uncertain.

Then I need confidence that the car will get me there. I need a sound engine, and faith in the guidance I'm following. I don't have to know everything about the vehicle to trust it to do what it's designed to do.

Only then does direction matter—the route, the timing, the next turn. Direction is not about speed. It's about orientation. It's knowing how to move forward without urgency or panic.

My goal is to help you develop all three:

- Clarity that lets you see where you are.
- Direction that empowers you to know where you are going.
- Confidence that allows you to trust your plan for how you will get there.

When those three things are aligned, we feel calm on the drive. If one is missing, even a short trip can feel stressful.

In my experience, some people lack this alignment. Without it, capable people feel stuck when they should be most confident. Though they live in a new season, their financial story gets stuck in the old assumptions.

Your Financial Story Didn't Start with You

Your financial story started before you can remember. Clarity doesn't judge that story. It recognizes truth and simplifies things. Many things shaped your unique mindsets around work, security, risk, responsibility, and worth. It started with what you saw your parents and grandparents, aunts and uncles, even teachers or people in your community model during stressful or celebratory moments.

Those who grew up during the Depression pass along a spendthrift mindset. They pick up every penny, and no matter how much they save, they never think it's enough. Regardless of how much they have in the bank, they feel broke. People who carried responsibility early often feel guilty enjoying what they've built. Those praised for being strong have a hard time admitting they feel uncertain.

Your feelings aren't wrong, but they are worth noticing.

Everyone has financial beliefs, things we take away from impressionable and impactful events in our lives. These moments mold us, and we use them to propel us forward. Clarity doesn't come from pushing harder, and it doesn't mean you know every thing. It comes from paying attention to patterns, outcomes, and the quiet beliefs that have shaped your behavior for decades. And it means that the noise begins to fade, so the next right thing becomes visible.

> **CLARITY DOESN'T COME FROM PUSHING HARDER. IT COMES FROM PAYING ATTENTION.**

Step Into Reality

Breaking the bonds of childhood mindsets is difficult, even after you become aware of them. To resolve the issue, each person needs to ask themselves a few questions:

- Why do I believe this (that I should save or that I have permission to spend)?
- Is my belief based on truth or on an impression my childhood made?

Many times, we hang on to what we know because it's comfortable, not because it's the healthiest thing for our relationships or even our own spending habits.

One of the most powerful moments I witness is when someone sighs with relief, "Oh, this makes sense now." It's not because they understand the numbers better, but because they understand how the story changed the numbers.

More than once, I've talked to someone who wants a new vehicle, but he feels like he can't afford it, even though, as I look in his accounts, he has more than enough to purchase a vehicle and continue to live comfortably. When that happens, I tell the person, "That's okay, your kids won't have any problem spending your money when you're not here."

Sometimes, that short message can help people see that not being able to afford it is a mindset, not the truth.

If you tell yourself, "I can't. I haven't saved enough. I can't afford to do those things," look at the math, and see if it tells you otherwise.

When I started in this business more than thirty years ago, we had an older neighbor who struggled. As a young couple, we helped him when we could. Then, one year, I did his taxes for him. The amount he claimed on his return shocked me. I remember thinking, *How can his mindset be so far off from reality?*

Be the Hero of Your Own Story

I wrote this book because I want you to see your retirement as an adventure, not a finish line, with you as the hero. It's not about perfection or performance. It's about alignment—understanding where you are, what matters most in this season, and how to make thoughtful decisions that support both your future and your well-being today.

The hero in every story starts the quest by gaining clarity. He or she wants to know the truth of the situation to gain confidence and respond in everyone's best interest. This confidence gives direction—not to an end, but to the next spot in the adventure.

Regardless of where you are in the story-building phase, it's not too late to realize you are the author. Heroes start with what they have and move forward. They don't worry about what they haven't done to prepare. They see the potential for adventure and go for it.

Dan Sullivan, co-founder of Strategic Coach®, has a phrase I love: "Always make your future bigger than your past." You have the power to make tomorrow bigger than today. Your hero's journey is like a measuring tape. Every day you have one inch less than the day before, so today is the perfect day to begin.

It doesn't matter where you came from or what you're doing right now; you can prepare for a bigger future. Some people in law enforcement feel lost when they lay down the gun and the badge. Because of the demands, many first responders leave the job after twenty years; however, that means they have a lot of time left before they actually retire. Being a trooper or a police officer had been their dream since they were a small child. None entered the profession for the money. But when they start thinking about a second career, the roadmap gets blurry. It's easy to forget retirement isn't a destination; it's just a mile marker on the way to a bigger future.

TO BE THE HERO OF YOUR OWN STORY, YOU CAN'T KEEP LOOKING AT THE PAST.

To be the hero of your own story, you can't keep looking at the past. John Glenn could have fallen victim to past thinking. After all, where do you go after you orbit the Earth? He imagined a bigger future and dedicated the rest of his life to public service as a United States Senator.

My wise husband understood he couldn't keep looking backward after his retirement from law enforcement. He started looking forward and planned for a bigger future.

Happy Desirement

As you move into your season of adventure, it's essential to remember retirement is not the destination. Retirement is the journey. It's not about sitting around and doing nothing; it's about transitioning and transforming.

It's what my friend Chad T. Jenkins, in his book *The Code to Collaboration,* calls achieving "a Desirement Lifestyle™." Chad said he realized conventional retirement just wasn't in his DNA. So, he began to focus on what he would do when he had the ability to do whatever he wanted. Instead of retiring, Chad wants to release his full potential and live out his passions, to do whatever he desires, and do it today—to spend time in Desirement.

YOUR ONE FINANCIAL LIFE[IP]

Every financial decision affects another because you only get One Financial Life[IP].

Regardless of which path you take, I want your retirement to become a Desirement Lifestyle. Rather than the focus of your retirement, money becomes your tool to achieve whatever you desire. This tool fuels every part of your One Financial Life: your purpose, estate, taxes, investment, income, insurance, health, family, and legacy. Understanding how these areas all work together makes your Desirement Lifestyle possible.

Cue the Confetti

I love confetti and glitter. I'll use any excuse to celebrate. And I believe our roadmap should include spots for merriment along the way. Throughout the book, I'm going to share Confetti Moments, places for you to pause and celebrate.

This book is meant to be more than a manual or workbook. I want to provide you with tools that will give you Clarity, Direction, and Confidence to help you recognize that birthdays matter more than balances.

Every moment of awareness is confetti-worthy. When you begin to see how your parents' mindsets influenced yours or start to be more intentional about envisioning your future, you should celebrate.

If this chapter felt calm rather than celebratory, that's intentional. I don't want to rush you forward; I want to help you see clearly, without blame or pressure, and without pretending the past didn't shape you. Because once you can see clearly, confidence grows, and when confidence grows, direction becomes possible.

This is the moment the realization settles in—that the story shaping these decisions was never consciously chosen. Consider for a moment:

- If my financial life were a story, would I want the next chapter to look like the last one?
- Whose beliefs about money have shaped my decisions more than my own?

Your financial story didn't start with you, but you get to decide how the next chapter is written.

2

The Illusion of "I'm Doing Fine"

Your future depends on what you do today.
—Gandhi

Your word is a lamp to my feet and a light to my path.
—Psalm 119:105 ESV

Over the years, I've learned that many people don't come to me because they lack intelligence, discipline, or effort. They come because something feels heavy. What they're really missing isn't another strategy—it's Clarity, Direction, and Confidence.

Clarity lets you understand where you are without judgment.

Direction shows you the next right step—without urgency or fear.

Confidence allows you to trust the plan guiding you forward.

When these three are aligned, decisions feel lighter. When one is missing, even good choices feel stressful.

Without paying attention to these three aspects, we get lulled into "I think we're doing fine."

I've heard those words more times than I can count, usually with a small pause before or after, just enough to suggest the speaker hopes the words are true.

"Fine" is a polite, non-confrontational word. It allows us to move on without opening anything up. It's also one of the most effective ways people unintentionally silence the questions that matter most because fine is not the same as clear.

Many who say they're doing fine have done everything they were supposed to. They showed up. But even though they appear to be prepared, they still feel unsettled. They worry they'll run out—run out of money, options, flexibility, and time.

The fear isn't necessarily irrational. It's often rooted in wisdom. But what some people sense isn't a shortage of money; it's a lack of coordination. Many households don't have a plan; they have accounts—a retirement account here, a bank account there, an old insurance policy in a drawer. Each piece may be handled responsibly, but when they don't communicate with each other, uncertainty grows, even when balances are strong. This is why objectively "fine" leads to anxiety.

Clarity Brings Confidence

I felt Linda faced financial uncertainty because she waited until retirement age to set up her roadmap. At our first meeting, Linda and I slowly went through her folder. Together, we looked at her Social Security timing, Medicare options, and her income gap. Page by page, we explored her spending needs and reviewed her 401(k) and Roth savings.

Linda came into my office believing she was fine, yet fearful she hadn't done enough. But as we made our way through her perfectly organized collection of papers, her shoulders relaxed, and her breathing slowed. She had made small, regular contributions to her 401(k) and never left matching funds on the table. But because she didn't know which investments were best and hadn't tracked the market, she had only assumptions rather than clarity.

As we ended our meeting, I showed Linda her income map—a clear, simple year-by-year picture of exactly how she could retire confidently. She studied it, and tears filled her eyes. "No one ever told me I was on the right track. I needed to hear the truth." She started to see that what she saw as "I did my best" was, in fact, "enough."

I'm Doing Fine

Linda's story, though unique to herself, might represent the majority of retirees. Teachers, nurses, office managers, receptionists, postal workers, bookkeepers, customer service reps, small-town heroes, and hardworking people everywhere need to step into the truth. I have discovered that many times, people have done better than they realize when they begin to examine their retirement financing.

Unfortunately, this "I'm Doing Fine" mindset creates fragmentation. It leaves important questions unanswered:

THIS "I'M DOING FINE" MINDSET CREATES FRAGMENTATION.

- When can we spend without fear?
- What needs to happen before we do?
- Which decisions are time-sensitive?
- What happens if something unexpected shows up?

In my opinion, the answers to these questions may help move the illusion of fine to the realm of confidence. If you want to make thoughtful decisions rather than reactive ones, you need to understand that life doesn't arrive neatly. Health changes, market shifts, family needs, job transitions, and other opportunities don't wait until everything feels perfect, and each one affects the others. When we don't consider timing ahead of time, even good decisions feel rushed, and the myth of fine begins to break down quietly.

Yes, Linda and others with their own unique circumstances may find themselves pleasantly surprised to learn they'll have enough to retire. Yet, in my experience, many more discover they could have done better if they had structure undergirding their decisions. This structure is difficult to build when everything lives in separate silos. Viewing the areas as your One Financial Life allows you to plan more efficiently.

The Year-Round Planner

For many years, clients only consulted me in February, March, and April—when it was time to do their taxes. Inevitably, that's when I found out they received a Required Minimum Distribution (RMD) or that their broker had sold some of the assets without considering gains or losses.

Another frustration came in when we discovered trusts that had never been funded, or the beneficiaries on their investment accounts didn't match their estate documents. Many people don't realize how insurance payouts and refunds of premiums can negatively impact their tax returns.

Every year at tax time, I felt like I was the one left holding the bag. Looking at a year's worth of deposits and withdrawals, I could see the problems, but the uncoordinated effort meant there was no one to pull it all together. It was up to me to inform the client that some of their money was in a higher tax bracket or that their Medicare premiums would increase in two years due to their current year's income.

The frustration of constantly being the bearer of bad news sent me back to school to become a Certified Financial Planner. Becoming a dual-licensed planner enabled me to provide my clients with informed recommendations in July and December. We don't focus on taxes only at tax time; we make changes based on the tax laws every day of the year. My firm also obtained its insurance license to alleviate that burden, and we work with an attorney consultant to ensure our estate planning is properly set up.

Your planners do not have to be together in one house; however, to avoid fragmentation and take advantage of tax laws and other considerations, you need tax, financial, and estate planners who will work together with one coordinator. It's my belief that the financial planner will be most ready to take up this mantle.

Unease Is Not Failure

FEELINGS OF INSECURITY ARE SIGNALS TO TALK TO THE PROFESSIONALS.

If you feel unsure of your future, you don't need to feel like a failure. You aren't alone. Even Clarity, Direction, and Confidence won't keep us from worrying about what lies ahead, especially when we encounter detours. Health, family situations, divorce, deaths, births, and other considerations all hold the potential to take us off course. Sometimes, hitting a milestone birthday will make us suddenly afraid that we haven't planned enough yet. However, none of these mean failure; instead, the feelings of insecurity these things inspire are signals to talk to the professionals who manage our accounts.

Clarity helps us know we'll always be on track, even during those months or years where the adventure takes us off-roading.

If you've ever thought, *I should feel better than this by now*, you're not alone. That thought doesn't mean you're ungrateful or irresponsible. It often means your life has shifted into a new season, and the old assumptions no longer fit. There's a difference between being financially "fine" and feeling financially secure.

Security is not just about having enough; it's about knowing how the pieces work together, knowing what comes next, and knowing that you don't have to make every decision perfectly or all at once.

For some people, the question isn't whether they've done enough; it's whether your decisions are connected to each other, your values, and the life you desire. You probably don't need more effort, just more coordination. Clarity doesn't come from tightening your grip; it comes from coordination, from stepping back and looking at the whole picture.

This is the moment the illusion of "I'm doing fine" starts to crack—not because something is wrong, but because you're noticing something deeper.

- Am I saying I'm fine because everything is truly aligned—or because I don't want to open the door to harder questions?

- What would change if I replaced "I'm doing fine" with "I want to be clear"?

Cue the Confetti

To me, Linda's confetti moment came when she felt an added peace of mind, pride, and gratitude for the lifetime of quality choices she had made. Though she had passed several milestones before she came into my office, the clarity she found gave her the confidence to step into the next season with dignity, purpose, and joy.

In their book, *The Gap and the Gain*™, Dan Sullivan and Dr. Benjamin Hardy encourage us to stop measuring backward. "Unsuccessful people focus on the Gap," the places where we feel like we fall short. "Successful people focus on the Gain," the progress they've made.[2]

Finding the right advisor can open the door for many more confetti moments. You don't need complexity; you need reassurance. Like Linda, you probably don't need a windfall; you need a roadmap. You aren't interested in living bigger; you want to live well.

It's time to celebrate your progress. Every time you take a step forward, cue the confetti.

Did you give yourself permission to purchase something you usually would have denied yourself because of the lessons you learned as a child? Cue the confetti.

Did you put an extra fifty dollars in your investment account rather than fear not having enough? Cue the confetti.

Maybe you reached the midpoint in your project or filed the paperwork for your business. Whatever progress you made this week, it's time to pull the cord, drop the balloons, and cue the confetti.

3

The Five Forces That Shape Everyday Life

Forces beyond your control can take away everything you possess except one thing, your freedom to choose how you will respond to the situation.
—Viktor Frankl

The prudent see danger and take refuge, but the simple keep going and pay the penalty.
—Proverbs 27:12

What if I told you that a good deal of financial stress doesn't come from a lack of intelligence or effort, but a lack of balance? Much of the unease people feel about their financial future is the result of forces pulling in different directions at the same time.

I've learned to look at every financial life through the lens of The Five Forces:

- Income
- Risk
- Liquidity
- Taxes
- Legacy

Regardless of income, profession, or net worth, when one of these areas is managed in isolation, it creates pressure. However, I believe, when they are aligned, people feel calm and oriented. Imbalanced, they make even good decisions feel heavy. These forces exist whether you're aware of them or not. But when you begin to see them clearly, you can coordinate them intentionally.

Income: The Stability Beneath the Surface

When I say income, some people think paycheck; however, it's more than that. Income gives you confidence because of its continuity. Income is knowing the reliability of any funds you have coming in and knowing how it will change over time.

MAILBOX MONEY SHOWS UP CONSISTENTLY.

My firm often refers to retirement income as "mailbox money." These are funds that show up consistently. They are sustainable and coordinated, so if this mailbox money is designed correctly, you should not outlive it, and if you are married, my firm also helps design your mailbox money in such a way that your spouse should not outlive it either.

That's how I evaluate income stability—not by optimism, but by durability.

Income stability also requires something else: keeping up with inflation. An income stream that never adjusts for the costs of living can quietly lose ground over time. What feels sufficient at the beginning of retirement may feel tight a decade later if it doesn't keep pace.

True income confidence accounts for both durability and purchasing power—not just whether income arrives, but whether it continues to support the life you're living as prices, healthcare costs, and expectations change.

I've met people with high incomes who feel anxious every month, and people with modest incomes who sleep well at night. The difference isn't the number. It's whether income is coordinated with lifestyle, spending, inflation, and future expectations.

To me, income doesn't need to be perfect. It needs to be dependable enough to support life as it is and as it's becoming.

Risk: How Much Are You Willing to Carry?

People often treat risk like a personality trait.

"You're conservative."

"You're aggressive."

"You can handle volatility."

But risk isn't about personality labels; It's about capacity—your emotional, financial, and seasonal capacity.

The same person can tolerate risk very differently at different stages of life. What felt acceptable at 40 can feel unsettling at 60. That isn't weakness. It's wisdom.

Risk needs to be matched to income needs, time horizon, and emotional tolerance. Mismatched risk means people lose trust, not just in markets, but in themselves. Risk should support confidence, not test it.

THOUGHTFULLY ALIGNED RISK LETS PEOPLE START TO TRUST THEIR DECISIONSAND STOP BRACING FOR IMPACT.

Thoughtfully aligned risk lets people start to trust their decisions and stop bracing for impact.

Liquidity: The Freedom to Act

We rarely discuss liquidity. We don't even notice it until it's missing. Liquidity gives you the ability to respond, say yes, and handle change without panic. It creates margin.

And margin creates additional peace of mind.

When they lock away too much of their finances, people feel trapped. Even the wealthy need liquidity because when we thoughtfully maintain our liquidity, life feels flexible.

Liquidity doesn't mean idle money; it means some portion of your investments is accessible without penalties. To feel confident about your financial situation, you need clarity about your options to access your funds in an emergency. Liquidity is one of the most underappreciated and most powerful forces.

Taxes: The Quiet Force That Shapes Outcomes

Paying unnecessary taxes is one common, preventable way retirement plans quietly erode.

After decades of watching good plans succumb to this by poor coordination, I became disciplined about one non-negotiable standard: clients should never pay more in taxes than the law requires—and that outcome should be intentional, not accidental.

We usually treat taxes as a yearly nuisance, but what if I told you they are really a lifelong force? Taxes influence nearly every decision—income, investments, timing, withdrawals, and legacy. Over a lifetime, they are often one of the largest expenses a family will ever face.

What matters most isn't how much you make. It's how much you keep. And one of the things that causes people to overpay is tax planning that is disconnected from everything else. When decisions are made in silos, taxes are rarely handled advantageously.

I don't encourage people to employ clever tricks, but with coordination, timing, and order, you have excellent tax efficiency and greater confidence. When we ignore thoughtfully integrated tax planning in our financial roadmap, regret often follows.

David and Karen Mitchell were the heart of their family—steady, kind, faithful, and always there when someone needed them. When I met them, they were preparing to celebrate their fortieth anniversary. Their three children and four grandchildren loved them dearly.

When we sat together to plan their retirement, they emphasized the importance of having funds for elder care if needed. They were prepared to live modestly to have money set aside. They weren't prepared for some of the tax rules that affected some of their retirement funds.

Like many people, David and Karen focused on taxes when they bought their new calendars. So, when I brought up taxes at our retirement planning meeting and suggested year-round planning, it took them by surprise.

With more than 9,000 sections and countless codes in each one, the United States tax law is the most complicated in the world. And every significant mile marker along our journey has unique laws about how we handle our buckets.

Karen had inherited IRAs from both her parents. As I explained the IRS 10-Year Rule for IRAs and the Required Minimum Distributions, Karen's eyes swelled. She would have to withdraw a portion of the IRAs each year and withdraw all within ten years. For some, this extra income can put them in a higher tax bracket. "I didn't expect to inherit responsibility," Karen lamented.

Like many in her position, Karen felt the mixture of grief after losing her parents and worry as she managed what they left behind.

We started the planning by using a strategy I call "Aligning Hearts before Numbers." We determined their deepest concerns and created a roadmap according to what weighed heaviest on their hearts. Some people don't realize that finding clarity in these areas can make it easier to create a financial plan for your future.

After we helped them better align their hearts, we were able to dive into their retirement roadmap. Armed with the full picture of their accounts, their goals, and the way the tax laws would impact their investments, we set out to prepare a plan that would help them navigate the next five to ten years.

The tax laws offer as many different routes for your retirement accounts as there are roads into Houston. By leveraging each one, we created a plan to help them have the greatest tax advantage possible. And every penny you save on your taxes can be money added to your retirement dollars.

Legacy: What Remains and What It Costs Others

Legacy problems rarely come from poor values. I believe they come from outdated paperwork, silence, and delay. I believe a simple habit can make an enormous difference. An intentional and regular beneficiary audit can give you added confidence and give your loved ones additional peace of mind after you're gone, knowing your wishes are being carried out. For many families, tying that review to birthdays becomes a meaningful reminder of another year lived and another opportunity to confirm alignment.

One family told me they never knew when to "check in" on their plan. Life felt busy, and nothing seemed urgent. We decided to use birthdays as a pause point. It became a moment for annual reflection. Over time, it turned into a rhythm. Their plan didn't feel heavy anymore. It felt cared for, as did their family.

Legacy also depends on having a completed, signed, and legally valid estate plan, executed according to the laws of the state where you live. Documents that are incomplete, unsigned, or created under old state laws can lead to confusion, disappointment, and unnecessary legal expense.

If you move, it matters. Your documents should move with you, legally and intentionally. An annual review will help you ensure your plans align with the laws in your new state.

And just as important as what's written is how your assets are designed to transfer. Probate should not be the default plan. When probate becomes the method of choice—usually by omission—families often inherit delays, costs, and stress at exactly the moment they are least prepared to handle it.

A THOUGHTFUL LEGACY DOESN'T JUST PASS ALONG ASSETS; IT PASSES ALONG CLARITY.

A thoughtful legacy doesn't just pass along assets; it passes along clarity.

Planning to Use The Five Forces to Your Advantage

Your plan has to take a step beyond dreaming to become a reality. When spouses plan for retirement, they have to take this one step further and plan for WE time. What do WE want to do together? What do WE really want to make time for and put on the calendar? Jim and Laura Dalton were headed for Alaska. Their plan included a great deal of dedicated WE time!

If you have friends or family you want to spend time with, your dream phase needs to expand to US time, and your calendar needs to reflect it. What do you want to do with your children, your friends, or your extended family?

What's not planned rarely happens. Intention is key to making sure your dreams come true.

Your calendar is probably the easiest thing to coordinate as you prepare for retirement. But how do things look for your retirement plan, long-term health care, and other life forces? The Financial Planning Mindset Scorecard^{IP} you'll find in the appendix and at www.beyondthemoneybo-ok.com can help you evaluate your readiness.

When I ask people if they have a retirement plan, many say they have a 401(k) or IRA. However, those are not retirement plans. Though obsolete, company-funded and owned pensions offer a "plan." They promise a monthly check for a specified amount. Sadly, many retirees don't realize until it's too late that their pension doesn't have a spousal benefit after their death.

On the other hand, 401(k)s and IRAs are accounts where you save your assets. Retirement Readiness means you have a plan to turn those accounts into income, and this can be the greatest challenge, depending on your dreams and your mindset.

A financial planner can help you develop a written plan that considers your entire life savings and sets it up as an income stream. If you've worked in more than one company, you might have several accounts. Your retirement plan will help determine where you take the money from.

Without a plan, you'll be grabbing out of buckets that could negatively impact the taxes you owe. Better financial planners should know how to pull from the tax now, tax later, or tax never buckets strategically, so you can keep your total income in your lowest possible bracket. Income readiness is more than just how much money your plan sends you each month; it's about how much you have left after taxes.

When Assets Drift: The Cost of "Lazy Money"

There's another force that quietly undermines even well-intentioned plans. I call it lazy money. It doesn't happen because people are careless, but because they invest and forget. It's found in accounts opened years ago, beneficiaries named in a different season of life, and investments left on autopilot while factors that affect the original decisions change.

One couple I met came in confident they were "in good shape." They worked hard, saved consistently, and updated their wills years earlier.

However, they never revisited the beneficiary designations on accounts they held through prior employers and inheritance. Nothing was technically wrong. But nothing was coordinated either. As we walked through their accounts together, they realized parts of their plan reflected who they used to be, not the life they were living now.

This is a highly misunderstood reality in planning: named beneficiaries and asset titles will often override estate documents and sometimes tax intentions as well.

LAZY MONEY ISN'T ABOUT POOR RETURNS. IT'S ABOUT MONEY THAT'S NO LONGER ALIGNED.

Lazy money isn't about poor returns. It's about money that's no longer aligned. And misalignment rarely announces itself. Without regular checks, these accounts will lie dormant, like a bear in hibernation.

Cue the Confetti

Three decades of experience have proven one thing to me: You can do very well in three or four of these areas and still feel unsettled if one is out of alignment. That doesn't mean you've failed. It means something important hasn't been seen yet.

Once people begin to understand how income, risk, liquidity, taxes, and legacy interact, something shifts. Hopefully, they stop asking, "Am I doing enough?" And start asking, "Does this work together?"

This is the moment where things feel heavy—not because you've failed, but because one or more of these forces may be out of alignment. Ask yourself:

- Which of The Five Forces feels most unsettled in my life right now?
- What would change if I stopped trying to manage everything separately and started bringing it together?

When confidence begins to form, it is not usually because everything is solved, but because clarity lets you trust the process that guides your next steps. It's also the moment to cue the confetti.

When you begin to understand where you are and how these forces work together to shape your One Financial Life, direction stops feeling urgent and starts to feel possible.

Part II: Designing Your One Financial Life – Direction

Where You Are Going

Once you understand your One Financial Life, you can begin intentionally designing where you want it to go.

4

Retirement Is Not a Date

Don't judge each day by the harvest you reap but by the seeds that you plant.
—Robert Louis Stevenson

For everything there is a season, and a time for every matter under heaven.
—Ecclesiastes 3:1 ESV

After we gain clarity, we are better able to choose our direction. Clarity reveals our current location; direction tells us where we are going. It has nothing to do with speed or distance; it allows us to take steps forward—small, deliberate actions. Your goal in your financial journey is constant forward motion.

Like deciding on the route for your next vacation, planning the direction of your retirement is a mix of art and science. We all share a few fixed markers—birthdays and milestone ages. Those are the science. We have no control over whether or when they come.

On the other side of the coin, however, we see the many different routes that will take us where we want to go. Choosing between the most scenic or direct route is more of an art. The place where science and art converge is a place where Clarity, Direction, and Confidence can potentially be found.

For example, the HR department where you work may look at retirement as an isolated date on their calendar—as science—but it's really much more. That simple date represents the beginning of one of the seasons of life, a life we navigate with art. Retirement is one of the final chapters in The Four Seasons of Financial Planning™.

The Seasons of Youth

Farmers understand the impact of seasons better than the average person. Spring and Summer are costly. Seed and gas for the tractors, as well as hours of planting, become an investment in their future. Financially, my firm calls Spring the Season of Accumulation and Opportunity.

Every season has its own prioritizations, and in the Spring of Life, my firm believes accumulation should top the list. It's vital not to miss any opportunities. The employer match may be one of the easiest opportunities to take advantage of. Bypassing it is as if you walked past an envelope with 3% of your paycheck in it every payday. And when you add the power of compounding to the full 6%, you leave thousands of retirement dollars on the table when you wait until Summer to start saving for retirement.

If you begin making retirement investments at twenty-five, you could stop before you turn forty and have more money in your retirement account at age sixty-six than the person who waited until they were forty to begin. Yes, compounding has the ability to work that hard for you.

People in the Spring of Life often have to learn the difference between wants and needs. The question, "Can I live without this?" becomes pivotal.

Like a farmer, you might work longer hours to make ends meet in the Spring. This is not a season of comfort; it's a season of accumulation and taking advantage of your youth and other opportunities.

The Summer of Financial Planning is the season of growth and stewardship. During the Summer, you watch your investments compound and increase your retirement contributions. This is the perfect time to build an emergency fund, your safety net, that will cover three to six months of your expenses.

If you haven't invested in life insurance, Summer is the time. The younger you start, the lower rate you can lock in. If you think you can't afford life insurance, imagine what would happen to your family if you weren't here. Who will bear your funeral expenses if something unforeseen happens? Stay-at-home moms should consider what it would cost to pay a caregiver if she weren't around.

By the time you exit your summer season, you could potentially have a six-figure retirement account. But you'll also want to make sure your student loans are paid off, and you have as little debt as possible.

DON'T NEGLECT YOUR HEALTH OR RELATIONSHIPS.

Beyond the money, you don't want to neglect your health or relationships during the Spring and Summer. You're young; working tons of overtime makes sense; however, investing in your health will make just as much difference in your retirement season as investing in your IRAs. Additionally, your Summer will be Winter for some of the people you love most. You don't want to spend so much time preparing for Fall and Winter that you miss your grandparents' or parents' final days. Understanding your values becomes essential as you maneuver through these early seasons.

Faith, Family, and Purpose Become Our Anchors

Though Strategic Coach only works with high-level entrepreneurs, I believe many of Dan Sullivan's principles transfer to general life. Dan and his team spend a great deal of time helping their clients find clarity. They guide them through a process that helps them discover their Unique Ability®, their purpose, and their highest values.

When my firm started running on EOS® (Entrepreneurial Operating System®), we realized the values we had stated for our business weren't made nearly clear enough for us. We narrowed our focus to four concise statements: Do the Right Thing, Get it Done, Be Coachable, and Maintain Positivity. Developing that clarity allowed us to hire the right people and attract the right clients. But they can be just as powerful in your personal life.

Everyone has strong values, but few take time to define them on a personal level. Without definition, it's easy to make plans that don't align with your true self. When it comes to faith, many people say, "I have time." However, if you wait, you may find decisions you make in the Spring and Summer of life don't align with a faith you define later.

YOUR CORE VALUES MAKE UP THE FOUNDATION OF WHO YOU ARE.

Discovering your three to seven core values helps you understand the foundation of who you are. Uncovering these simple words or phrases will not only help you understand yourself better, but you'll find they have been driving your behavior for years. They are your moral compass, but like any navigational tool, if you don't understand how to use it or know it's there, it will be pointless. Values undefined push you along like a boat with a broken rudder and a strong wind in the sails. You will be in constant motion, but

the direction might feel aimless at times.

That's why I call faith, family, and purpose the anchors of our life. Identifying your values and deciding how you want them to influence your behavior helps set guardrails so you stay on the route you've laid out for yourself. For instance, grandparents with a loosely defined value of family might find themselves raising their grandchildren. By clearly defining how that goal will drive behavior, those same grandparents may position themselves to better live out their value of charity by going on mission trips.

The beautiful thing about developing clarity around what you value most is the way it can help you as you write your story and map out your adventure. Your faith, family, and purpose become anchors that will keep you from drifting off your plan. It's these values that will encourage you to make time for your loved ones while trying to build your retirement accounts.

Building a Spring and Summer based on these anchors can set you up for an easy harvest.

Harvest and Transition, Legacy and Peace of Mind

Even in Florida, we can't stop the leaves from falling off the maple trees. Seasons pass without our permission, and so do those milestone birthdays. Like the weather transitions from Summer to Fall, your transition to retirement might not be as clean as a date on the calendar. Some will move into golfing, pickleball, or vacations; others transition into a more prominent grandparent role. However, for many first responders and entrepreneurs, this season turns into consulting, finding a second career, or serving the business in a different capacity. That's why I love the concept of Desirement—transitioning into the life you most desire.

If you missed those Spring and Summer investments, now is not the time to feel bad. Some people's health issues keep them from being where they want to be financially. Others have faced divorce or downsizing. We can't control the detours on our journey, but we can control the reroute. During our Fall, our lives shift from accumulation to intention.

I've had people ask me if they should pay off their mortgage before they retire. Science looks at the mortgage rate. I know people who only pay 2.5% on their house loan, so taking money that's earning 6% or more each year to pay off the house doesn't make sense. However, the art involved needs to review your unique circumstances so you can be intentional about your decision.

Fall also gives you an opportunity to declutter. If you don't clean up your mess, someone else will have to. Is that the legacy you want to leave? In addition to cleaning out the attic and getting rid of those things no one wants, it's time to organize the important papers your loved ones will need after you're gone.

You will always be able to find someone who has saved more money than you have, but harvest and transition go way beyond the money. Your Winter funding should be just a matter of doing the math. But the kind of lifestyle you choose paints a picture that determines how you'll fund your Fall.

Like the farmer, we prepare for Winter throughout the other three seasons. The amount you invest in your health, your accounts, and your relationships will prove valuable when you reach Winter.

As you enter your final years, you'll probably start to slow down. A meeting between you, your estate planner, and your wealth advisor will prove invaluable. During the Winter, you can decide if you want to leave money to your family or charity or spend it all before you're gone. Now that you know how much is left, you can fine-tune your goals.

This is the perfect time to reevaluate your life insurance policies. Do you still need them? If you have enough in your accounts to pay for your funeral, and you don't have any family left to care for, you might want to see if your policies have cash value.

Depending on the prior seasons, some people may have to live more modestly. But I've encountered just as many who felt like they needed permission to spend what they have. I enjoy helping those who lived their Summer and Fall being such good stewards; they got used to being thrifty. I remind them that they can afford a bigger boat or a first-class plane ticket. Perhaps they don't want to spend it, but they shouldn't say "I can't afford it" anymore.

This is the moment I believe you should stop thinking about retirement as a finish line and start seeing it as a direction you're choosing, season by season. It's in the moment you should ask:

- Am I making decisions based on a date—or based on the life I want to live in this next season?
- What would change if I focused less on when I retire and more on how I want to live along the way?

Cue the Confetti

Too often, we confine retirement to a single date rather than a season to prepare for and move through. When we do, pressure builds, and transitions feel rushed.

But when we look at each small movement forward in every season as a step toward retirement, we realize every one deserves a little confetti. From signing up for your employer match to being intentional about how you live out your values or pay down your mortgage, each decision that strengthens your Fall and Winter is worth recognizing.

Next, I want to look at how timing—not just age—shapes the seasons ahead, and why certain moments quietly matter more than others.

5

Big Birthdays That Shape Your Financial Story

At twenty years of age, the will reigns; at thirty, the wit; and at forty, the judgment.
—Benjamin Franklin

Teach us to number our days, that we may gain a heart of wisdom.
—Psalm 90:12

I love birthdays, probably because I enjoy celebrations so much. In my family, we don't just have birthday celebrations; we have birth-month celebrations. In fact, I want others to enjoy their birthdays so much that sometimes I create birthday kits—a pretty bag with a cake mix and everything you need for the cake, plus candles, balloons, and confetti—which I donate to the local food pantry. Everyone deserves to enjoy birthdays as much as I do. Blame it on my mom; she got it all started. But the beauty of life is that when you live with Clarity, Direction, and Confidence, it's easier to celebrate the financial milestones along the way.

Birthday Milestones

Every birthday, including the day you were born, holds a milestone for life. However, a few celebration dates offer specific checkpoints for someone heading into the Fall or Winter of Life.

Penalty-Free Access Begins at Age 59 ½

Changes: For the first time, retirement accounts can be accessed without an early-withdrawal penalty. What once felt untouchable suddenly feels available.

What We See: Some people confuse access with readiness. They make withdrawals without understanding taxes, long-term income needs, or market timing risk.

What Matters Most: This birthday isn't about spending; it's about coordination. The Five Forces, especially income, taxes, and risk, are now better able to intersect with time.

Tools: 360° Retirement Roadmap[IP], Retirement Operating System[IP], and My When File[IP].

Quiet Planning Question: If you need income next year, where exactly should it come from and why?

Social Security Becomes Available at Age 62

Changes: You may begin collecting Social Security. This feels like a finish line, but it's actually a fork in the road.

What We See: Some people file for Social Security because they can, not because it fits their plan.

What Matters Most: This decision is permanent and impacts lifetime income and survivor benefits.

Tools: My firm utilizes Social Security Optimization within the 360° Retirement Roadmap, tax projection, and income coordination.

Quiet Planning Question: Are you claiming Social Security because it fits your plan, or because it feels familiar?

You May Enroll in Medicare Between the Ages of 64½ and 65

Changes: Healthcare officially becomes a financial decision.

What We See: Some people miss application deadlines, potentially facing penalties and surprises from Medicare's premium surcharges, the Income-Related Monthly Adjustment Amount (IRMAA).

What Matters Most: Healthcare costs are one of retirement's largest unknowns.

Tools: Medicare coordination, IRMAA awareness, cash-flow, and tax mapping.

Quiet Planning Question: Do you know what Medicare will actually cost you?

Full Retirement Age for Many Hits at Age 67

Changes: You may now be able to access your full Social Security Benefits.

What We See: Some people mistake this birthday for a universal retirement date.

What Matters Most: Knowing that retirement is not an age; it's an income strategy.

Tools: Income layering, Risk alignment reviews, Spousal coordination.

Quiet Planning Question: If work became optional tomorrow, would your income be ready?

Charitable Planning Opportunity Begins at Age 70½

Changes: Some people can begin making Qualified Charitable Distributions (QCDs).

What We See: Charitable giving remains inefficient.

What Matters Most: Giving can be intentional and tax-efficient.

Tools: QCD Planning, Charitable strategy integration

Quiet Planning Question: Could your generosity reduce your tax burden without changing what you give?

Required Minimum Distributions (RMDs)

Begin at Ages 72 (born before 1950), 73 (born 1951-1959), and 75 (born 1960 or later)

Changes: The IRS requires distributions from your IRA, whether you need the income or not.

What We See: Years of inaction surface as higher taxes and fewer options.

What Matters Most: RMDs punish reaction and reward preparation, something I've watched play out repeatedly over decades of tax planning.

Tools: RMD Strategy within the 360° Retirement Roadmap, tax bracket management, legacy and beneficiary coordination, My When File

Quiet Planning Question: If the IRS is setting the pace for your distributions, who is really in control?

A BIRTHDAY ISN'T JUST A CELEBRATION, IT'S A PLANNING SIGNAL.

Though this non-inclusive list just touches on the celebration mile markers, these marks on your roadmap give you a starting place to talk to your specialist. Remember, a birthday isn't just a celebration; it's a planning signal.

Big Birthdays Are Not Arbitrary. They are points where rules change, options appear, and consequences could begin to compound.

What matters is not the birthday itself, but what becomes possible, or restricted, on the other side of it.

Big Birthday Matrix[IP]

Age	Milestone	What It Triggers
Birth	Life Begins	Values, habits, and examples are formed
18	Legal Adulthood	Contracts, privacy, and legal responsibility
21	Full Legal Access	Independent financial decisions
25	Insurance Transition	Health coverage and early career choices
30	Accumulation Reality	Direction, debt, and saving habits
35	Competing Priorities	Family, protection, and planning discipline
40	Midlife Checkpoint	Alignment of goals, risk, and investments
45	Course Correction	Tax awareness and long-term strategy
50	Catch-Up Eligible	Higher retirement contribution limits
55	Early Access Options	Income bridge and benefit planning
59½	Penalty-Free Access	Retirement accounts become accessible
62	Social Security Eligible	Reduced benefits available
65	Medicare Begins	Healthcare becomes a financial decision
67	Full Retirement Age*	Full Social Security benefits (varies)
70½	Charitable Planning	Qualified Charitable Distributions available
72 / 73 / 75	RMDs Begin	Required distributions and tax management
80+	Legacy & Simplicity	Ease, clarity, and instructions for loved ones

Using Birthdays for Retirement Planning

Retirement planning is often built with good intentions. But with Required Minimum Distributions, intention may give way to obligation. Once RMD age is reached, withdrawals must begin, whether income is needed or not. And if you delay and take your distribution after April 1 of the year following the year you reach RMD age, you might face two taxable distributions in one year.

THE IRS DOESN'T CARE HOW THOUGHTFUL YOUR RETIREMENT IS; IT ONLY CARES WHETHER YOU FOLLOW THE RULES.

Poor timing and lack of coordination can trigger unnecessary taxes, higher Medicare premiums, and penalties that undo years of careful saving. As a CPA, I've seen how a single missed milestone year can quietly undo decades of disciplined saving—not because people were careless, but because no one helped them connect timing, taxes, and income. At certain birthdays, the risk isn't market loss; it's having the wrong money in the wrong place at the wrong time. The IRS rules are fixed, and the IRS doesn't care how thoughtful your retirement plan is; it only cares whether you follow the rules. Careful planning helps separate clarity from reaction.

Many jokingly say they quit having birthdays after forty or fifty; however, as far as tax planning goes, birthdays matter more than balances. Some people don't run into tax problems because they lack discipline; it generally stems from a lack of coordination. When you plan for these milestone years early, you'll have freedom when they roll around. Keeping it simple is a gift to your loved ones.

You are not late—retirement planning is not about when you start, but whether the next decision is the right one.

This is the moment birthdays stop feeling like just celebrations and start revealing themselves as decision points:

- Which upcoming birthday deserves more attention than I've been giving it?

- What would change if I treated that birthday as a planning signal instead of something to avoid or ignore?

Qualified Charitable Distributions

In order to reduce some of the tax burden on RMDs, I often recommend Qualified Charitable Distributions (QCDs). I ask, "What if you could save a few thousand tax dollars every year just by giving more money to the charities you already support?"

Depending on individual circumstances, after you reach your 70½ milestone, you might begin making donations to your favorite charity and exclude the entire amount from your taxable income. And that's in addition to the standard minimum deduction. The money has to go straight from your IRA to the charity, but if you have a Required Minimum Distribution (RMD) that puts you into the next tax bracket, giving all or a portion of it to a qualified charity could save you a great deal. The order of operations for this to be completed timely and accurately is important.

Sadly, some wealth managers may overlook QCDs because they're tax-focused, and many tax planners don't mention them because they involve extra tax paperwork and require coordination across advisors.

Big birthdays are more than milestones on a calendar. They are moments of convergence—when age, opportunity, responsibility, and consequence quietly meet. Decisions made around these turning points often feel ordinary at the time, yet they can shape the decades that follow. This is why timing matters as much as intention, and why clarity alone is not enough.

Before Growth, Protection

Before we talk about growth, income, or opportunity, there is something more important we would like to address—protection. I don't mean protection from the markets themselves, but protection from decisions made at the wrong time, under the wrong conditions, or without full awareness of their long-term impact.

After more than three decades of working with individuals and families through retirement transitions, I've learned something that may sound simple but is often overlooked: some people don't make reckless financial decisions. They make reasonable ones—just at the wrong moment. And the cost of those moments might not be visible right away.

That is where structure matters.

A true fiduciary relationship is not about predicting markets or choosing products. It is about one party owing another a duty of loyalty, care, and good faith. The fiduciary is required to act primarily in the interests of the other. They are responsible to protect people from risks they cannot easily see, especially when emotion, timing, or uncertainty clouds judgment. A good guide doesn't say yes to every idea. A good guide ensures that every decision respects the life it is meant to support.

The role of this book is to explain the thinking behind protection—not to recommend specific products or strategies. This is where guardrails come in.

Guardrails are not designed to be restrictions. Rather, they are protections—set up to keep one decision from unraveling everything else. Certain risks simply don't belong in the market. They belong behind stabilizers that allow the rest of the plan to function without interruption. This is where insurance and protection planning play a critical role—not as investments, not as strategies for return, but as tools that prevent forced decisions during vulnerable moments. Protection strategies vary by an individual's unique circumstances. They should be evaluated as part of a broader planning process.

I believe one misunderstood risk in retirement is the sequence of returns risk. It isn't about how much you earn over time—it's about when gains and losses occur. Two people can experience the same average return and end up with dramatically different outcomes based solely on timing. Losses early in retirement can potentially affect the material trajectory of a plan, not because the plan was flawed, but because withdrawals were required at the worst possible moment.

This is why, I believe, protection needs to be a priority at the beginning of retirement—not the end.

Guardrails exist so that market downturns do not dictate life decisions. They give people the ability to wait, recover, and remain intentional rather than reactive. Without them, even strong plans can be compromised by poor timing.

At the same time, protection does not mean paralysis.

Another quiet risk I see often is what I call lazy money—assets that sit idle not because it's strategic, but because no one has clarified their purpose. Money that isn't working intentionally isn't truly aligned with its intended purposes; it is quietly falling behind. Cash, reserves, and conservative assets all have jobs to do but only when they are aligned with time, purpose, and risk.

This balance matters.

Growth builds wealth.

Protection preserves freedom.

Timing determines whether either one works.

Even with a disciplined investment strategy, markets will not cooperate on your timeline. They do not respect retirement dates, health events, or family obligations. Some risk can be managed, diversified, and planned for, but it cannot be eliminated by hedging. And when the consequences of bad timing are too high, relying on investments alone places unnecessary pressure on a retirement plan that is meant to provide stability, not stress, in the years when reliability is meant to matter the most.

Insurance: Protection, Not Performance

Some tools prioritize certainty over growth; others favor flexibility over guarantees. That's why insurance is something to be considered when you plan for your One Financial Life. The right choice, for your unique set of circumstances, generally depends entirely on timing, purpose, and integration within the broader plan.

The Advantages

- Transfers risk that is too large or unpredictable to self-insure
- Creates certainty when timing matters
- Reduces pressure on investment portfolios during market downturns
- Protects independence, dignity, and family decision-making

The Disadvantages

- Ongoing costs that must be justified
- Complexity that can obscure true value

- Poorly structured policies can limit future flexibility
- Insurance chosen in isolation often solves the wrong problem

The framework you are about to see is designed to help you with these principles in mind. It doesn't chase performance or avoid risk blindly. It has the potential to create structure so that decisions can be made with clarity, confidence, and context—before emotion or urgency takes over.

I believe growth only belongs in the conversation after protection is established.

Cue the Confetti

Too many people wait until retirement to throw the party, but I think we need to stop at every mile marker and celebrate. Every decade deserves some confetti.

6

THE RETIREMENT OPERATING SYSTEM[IP]

Good order is the foundation of all great things.
—Edmund Burke

The heart of a man plans his ways, but the Lord establishes his steps.
—Proverbs 16:9 ESV

Protection creates the conditions for good decisions, but structure makes them repeatable.

By now, it's clear that timing, responsibility, and unseen risk matter just as much as intention. Insight brings awareness, but awareness alone doesn't create outcomes. What creates outcomes is order—a disciplined way to align decisions with purpose, time, and consequence before urgency takes over.

This is where the Retirement Operating System comes in. An operating system isn't a product or a checklist. It's a way of thinking—a framework that ensures income, investments, taxes, protection, and legacy work together rather than compete with one another. Without coordination, even good decisions can work against each other. With it, choices become clearer, tradeoffs become intentional, and confidence replaces guesswork.

The Retirement Operating System exists for one reason: to help people make decisions in the right order, at the right time, with the right guardrails in place. It reduces reaction, prevents forced moves, and preserves flexibility across seasons of life—not by predicting the future, but by preparing for it.

In the pages ahead, I will show you how this system brings clarity to complexity and direction to decisions, so confidence isn't something you hope for, but something you build.

The science of advising includes several "orders of operations." Parts of the journey just work better when we do them in the proper sequence. Your financial planning is like a math problem. Many of us remember the order of operations our math teachers tried to impress upon us: PEMDAS or Please Excuse My Dear Aunt Sally. They used the mnemonic device to help us remember that math problems require order:

Parentheses
Exponents
Multiplication and Division
Addition and Subtraction

People who don't follow the order of operations might think $9 - 6 \times 4 + 25 = 37$, but the correct answer is 10. At the same time, $9 - 6 \times (4 + 25) = -165$. Two problems with exactly the same numbers, but using order of operations correctly means different outcomes.

Life planning can be thought to work the same way. We can have the right tools, the right intentions, and the right goals, but without the correct sequence, we lose clarity. Decisions compete with each other, and progress feels scattered. If we lack direction, our confidence could erode, all because things have not been placed where they belong.

You see, this may be your first retirement, but it isn't mine. I've watched thousands unfold. And I've learned which choices inspire confidence and which quietly create regret. My perspective doesn't make me smarter, but it puts me in a position to help people avoid solving the wrong problem at the wrong time.

The Problem with Doing Everything at Once

Some people approach retirement planning as if everything needs to be solved immediately. This gives income, investments, taxes, healthcare, legacy, and lifestyle decisions equal urgency. The overwhelming nature of so many decisions causes people to freeze or move forward without confidence.

SOME PEOPLE DON'T NEED A BETTER STRATEGY; THEY NEED FEWER DECISIONS COMPETING FOR ATTENTION.

In my observations, few have a motivation or intelligence problem; they have an order problem. Replacing income requires different rules than accumulating assets. The same strategy rarely does both well at the same time. As people get older, risk stops being about market swings and starts being about whether income shows up when it's needed. Preservation and income replacement begin to matter more than pure growth. Some people don't need a better strategy; they need fewer decisions competing for attention.

When planning lacks order, everything feels unfinished. Even strong financial progress can feel temporary. The unease you feel doesn't mean something is broken. It's a signal that the plan isn't moving in the proper sequence.

Using the Retirement Operating System (ROS) creates steadiness and gives you the assurance that today's decisions belong where they are.

Prioritizing the Order of Operations can create relief. Rather than attempting to do everything at once, we ask one simple question: What needs my attention now, and what can wait? Understanding this reminds us not everything has to happen in a short window. We don't have to fit everything into a checklist; instead, we start to see things through the lens of a sequence.

In every stage, The Five Forces have the same order of operations:

- Income planning comes before investment risk.
- Liquidity precedes long-term commitments.
- Tax awareness falls ahead of irreversible decisions.
- Clarity goes before direction, and direction before confidence.
- And everything else before Legacy.

In the same way, each birthday builds on the last. Decade by decade, when we follow a sequence that prioritizes what needs our attention now, we no longer have to ask, "Am I doing enough?" The question turns to "Does this make sense right now?"

This type of question may stop the competition between decisions and help them start falling into place. This is also the point where investments stop being about performance and start being about purpose—what each dollar is meant to do, and when.

- What decision have I been trying to make too early—or too late?
- What would feel different if I trusted sequence instead of urgency?

The Three Buckets of Retirement Planning[IP]

We use The Three Buckets of Retirement Planning to demonstrate how the Order of Operations allows you to be intentional with your finances. Strategic investments help keep you from worrying about market swings and help us give your money the best opportunity to work for you.

These buckets allow you to avoid lazy money. Our goal is to let your funds earn as much interest as possible, while always having your immediate needs covered. Later, we'll look at tools designed to reduce downside risk and stabilize income, but only after we understand what each dollar is meant to do.

- **The Now Bucket** – This bucket prepares you for things you will need funds for in the next three years—monthly distributions, vacation, vehicles, house repairs, appliances, and other major purchases. This Bucket provides liquidity. We invest it so market volatility has less impact, because this money is meant for near-term income and known expenses.
- **The Soon Bucket** – We review buckets annually and prepare the Soon Bucket to refill the Now Bucket as needed. In a coordinated plan, funds intended for near-term needs are typical-

ly positioned with lower volatility and for measured growth—enough to replenish the Now Bucket without exposing income to unnecessary risk.

- **The Later Bucket** – This long-term growth bucket contains funds for expenses you anticipate in ten years or more. Because this money isn't needed soon, it can tolerate market swings and provide long-term growth to combat inflation. This structure allows income needs to be met without forcing long-term investments to be sold during market downturns.

We have seen too many people build an emergency fund that amounts to five times what an average family needs to survive for a year. In many cases, this results in hundreds of thousands of dollars sitting in checking or savings accounts, earning far less than their potential.

In farm life, unused resources don't quietly sit—they lose value. Seed left in the barn doesn't grow a harvest. Equipment left idle still rusts. Money has the potential to work the same way. When it isn't assigned a purpose, it may quietly fall behind. That's what I mean by lazy money. Lazy is a four-letter word, but in planning, it doesn't describe people. It describes money that hasn't been given a job.

The examples and frameworks in this book are meant to illustrate principles, not to replace individualized advice based on a person's specific circumstances.

Cue the Confetti

GOOD DECISIONS MADE OUT OF ORDER CREATE STRESS.

Good decisions made out of order create stress, while calm directions replace the guesswork. One of the saddest circumstances I encounter when I meet with people ready to retire is parents who still have debt because they're taking care of their adult children. This scenario emphasizes the importance of the Order of Operations. It's vital that we pay off our own high-interest obligations and set up our plan for our future before we pay bills for children who have graduated from college. If you feel bad because you can't help your kids, remind yourself they need to learn life's Order of Operations, too. Getting the Order of Operations right at a young age will help to better set them up for success. When the order is honored, we make financial decisions with calm, clarity, and more confidence. When it is ignored, even good decisions may end in regret.

In the Appendix, you'll find a breakdown of the Retirement Operating System by decade. In each season of your life, certain financial moves will take you in the direction of becoming the hero of your retirement. This means you're better positioned for a confetti shower every time you complete any of the five steps you'll find in that framework.

Retirement planning isn't a math problem; it's a timing issue. The Retirement Operating System restores discipline to decision-making. It doesn't make life rigid; it makes life work.

Part III: Living Your One Financial Life – Confidence

How You Get There

Living your One Financial Life isn't about achieving perfection. It's about making coordinated decisions that give you confidence through every season of life.

7

The Team Around the Table

Nothing is impossible for those who act after wise counsel and careful thought.
—Thiruvalluvar

Plans succeed with counsel, and with good advice make war.
—Proverbs 20:18

So far, we've looked at the importance of developing Clarity and Direction, knowing where you are and where you're going. You've started to become confident in your future. Confidence doesn't mean you have it all figured out. It means you trust the process and feel an assurance that lets you move forward without fear.

Even with a thoughtful plan in place, many people entering retirement feel unsettled. That feeling doesn't mean something is wrong. It means something important is changing.

Retirement is more than a financial transition. It's a shift in identity, rhythm, and trust. For decades, work provided structure, validation, and momentum. Decisions were reinforced by routine. Paychecks arrived on schedule. Progress felt measurable.

Retirement removes those familiar markers. Even when the math works, the mind looks for reassurance. It's common to second-guess decisions, hesitate longer than expected, or wonder whether confidence is supposed to feel stronger by now.

Confidence at this stage doesn't arrive all at once. It builds gradually through clarity, through order, and through repeated confirmation that today's decisions belong where they are. Feeling cautious doesn't mean you lack courage. It means you're more likely aware of what's at stake. The goal of good planning is not to eliminate emotion, but to keep emotion from driving timing.

This is where structure matters so much. A clear process allows confidence to grow without pressure. It helps give you permission to move forward thoughtfully, rather than urgently. When confidence is supported by sequence and guardrails, it becomes steady. And when confidence is steady, decisions may stop feeling heavy and start feeling right.

Order of Operations invites us to make sure we have a team in place to help us navigate our journey with confidence. Over the years, I've met many thoughtful, responsible people who were doing everything right. They may have had an investment advisor, a CPA, an attorney, all the correct insurance policies, employer plans, and records of all the accounts they had accumulated carefully over the decades.

Still, when we sat down together, I could sense their unease. No one had failed them; every piece had been handled appropriately. However, no one had put all the pieces together so they could see the entire picture.

Coordination Is Key

To me, people don't suffer from a lack of advice; advice is common. Instead, they suffer from a lack of coordination, because coordination is rare.

Long before conference rooms and financial software, this work began at my kitchen table. That's where people first trusted me with their questions—not technical ones, but human ones.

"Am I okay?"

"Are we missing something?"

"What happens if something happens to me?"

Those questions don't belong to any one profession. They belong to a conversation that includes listening, perspective, and the willingness to say, "We need someone else at the table for this part."

WHEN PROFESSIONALS WORK IN SILOS, GAPS HAVE THE OPPORTUNITY TO FORM QUIETLY.

When professionals work in silos, gaps have the opportunity to form quietly. Taxes get paid unnecessarily, beneficiaries go outdated, insurance overlaps or disappears, and estate documents don't match account registrations.

Decisions made in isolation may result in consequences that ripple elsewhere. Some of the regret I've seen in retirement didn't come from bad intentions or poor discipline; it came from decisions made without coordination. That's why I like to paint the picture of all the areas coming together in One Financial Life.

Good planning recognizes professional boundaries and respects the expertise each advisor brings.

The Added Peace That Coordination Brings

Jim Dalton served two tours in the Army right out of high school. When he came home, he followed the tug toward public service by becoming a firefighter.

Thirty years later, he was ready to step into a new chapter that didn't require running into burning buildings. But first, he wanted to make sure his wife of more than thirty years would be taken care of if something happened to him. "If something happens to me," he said, "I just want to know she'll be okay."

Jim wasn't chasing returns. He wasn't asking for complexity. He wanted reassurance for the person he loved most.

When I sat down with Jim and Laura, they gave me their dream list, and we compared it to The Five Forces. As we talked, it became clear that while Jim had accounts, professionals, and good intentions, no one had ever stepped back to look at how it all worked together—income, risk, taxes, liquidity, and legacy.

That's when I explained something gently but honestly: "No one person needs to know everything. But someone needs to see everything. And that someone must know when to bring the right people into the conversation."

For first responders in Florida, this coordination gap has the potential to show up clearly in programs like DROP and the Florida Retirement System. Some people are asked to choose between the Investment Plan and the Pension Plan, or to elect DROP benefits, without fully understanding how those decisions interact with taxes, survivor benefits, healthcare costs, or federal protections.

I've also seen confusion around benefits designed to support first responders injured in the line of duty, including protections provided under Heart and Lung laws.

Heart and Lung laws generally provide a presumption that certain injuries or illnesses—often related to cardiac, pulmonary, or stress-related conditions—are connected to public safety service. That presumption can allow qualifying first responders to receive continued income and medical benefits during recovery, rather than facing delays or reductions common in standard disability or workers' compensation processes. While eligibility and administration vary by state, these protections are intended to stabilize families at moments when work, health, and income are suddenly disrupted.

These laws exist for a reason, but they only work as intended when they're coordinated with retirement elections, income planning, and estate considerations. These aren't small decisions. Once made, many of them are difficult or impossible to reverse. That's why having the right people around the table at the right time matters so much.

While the rules differ by state and profession, the lesson is universal: benefits chosen in isolation often create unintended consequences later.

Jim had a special pension set up for first responders, and he qualified for additional benefits under Federal and Florida law. I connected him with an attorney who specializes in first responder benefits—someone who understood nuances Jim didn't even realize might apply to him.

Jim simply wanted to make certain his wife was protected, and by bringing the right team together, we did just that.

Coordinate for the People You Care About

Navigating the road to retirement can be as intimidating as traveling in a country where the steering wheel is on the right. With the mix of tax laws and investment options, it's easy to get overwhelmed regardless of the size of your account. Should I rollover, or leave my money where it is? When can I do a rollover? When can I take money out of my investments, and how much can I take? And if you're considering retirement, but your children still depend on your finances, you might think you'll never retire.

THE RIGHT GUIDES PAINT A PICTURE OF WHAT YOUR ADVENTURE MIGHT LOOK LIKE

The right guides paint a picture of what your adventure might look like based on your goals, values, and the funds you have available. And just like a river guide doesn't have the same skills as a mountain guide, you need a team of professionals with a variety of talents. Every story, including your individual circumstances, will have its own unique turns and twists. No two drawings will look the same.

Being the hero of your own story begins with finding the right guides—men and women who align with your values and care about your mission. These people will work together to make recommendations and show you the potential pitfalls. Plus, you want a team with a passion to make the story about you. You don't want to do what everyone else does.

Some people need an estate planning attorney, a tax planner, a wealth manager, and a retirement advisor. Ideally, you want one of these guides to be the coordinator. By bringing your professionals together as a team, even if your Summer and Spring were a bit rocky, you can create a Fall of great harvest.

A coordinated team doesn't replace expertise; it respects it. When I coordinate my clients' teams, I don't take on the role of hero. My purpose is to bring clarity and experienced judgment so people can make wise decisions and leave a better story behind.

That means knowing when to say:

"This is a tax question."

"This is a legal issue."

"This is about income, not investments."

"This is about added peace of mind, not optimization."

True confidence doesn't come from doing everything yourself. It comes from knowing the right people are involved at the right time and for the right reasons.

TRUE CONFIDENCE COMES FROM KNOWING THE RIGHT PEOPLE ARE INVOLVED.

This is the moment confidence stops feeling like something you have to manufacture and starts feeling like something you can trust.

- Who is currently helping me see the whole picture—not just one piece of it?
- What would feel different if I knew the right people were around the table for the right reasons?

Cue the Confetti

Many think they'll never be able to afford to retire, but I've discovered that sometimes, those doubts may come from comparisons. You hear a neighbor or a nephew talk about his or her retirement package and assume you don't have enough. Many people feel like they should throw some confetti when they see their financial picture after they gather a team and appoint one person to help them coordinate.

When you gather the right team around the table, something shifts. Conversations slow down, questions improve, and decisions feel lighter.

People turn the question from, "What product do I need?" to, "Does this work together?"

That's when confidence begins to form—not from certainty, but from trust. Trust in the process. Trust in the people. Trust that nothing important is being overlooked. That feeling of confidence means it's time to let off the cannons because you've paved the way for your family to move forward, not with perfection but with wisdom.

8

The 360° Retirement Roadmap

Study the past if you would divine the future.
—Confucius

Every prudent man acts with knowledge, but a fool flaunts his folly
—Proverbs 13:16 ESV

Uncertainty plagues even people who have done their best. Before we can feel confident, we need to see how everything fits together. Without that clarity, we hesitate, even if we've gathered a team and checked all the boxes. It's as if we stop at a crossroads and wonder which way to go next. That's why we need a roadmap.

The most powerful mindset shift I've seen in more than three decades of planning comes when someone finally understands how their entire financial picture—past, present, and future—works together. This confidence comes when we show them the full picture. That's the purpose of a 360° view.

Making the Connection

The 360° Retirement Roadmap begins by recognizing that at the center is a person, not a portfolio, a spreadsheet, or a projection. Around that person, we find the forces that quietly shape their decisions: income, risk, liquidity, taxes, and legacy, accompanied by health, timing, and intention. Handled individually, even good decisions in these areas may stress the other forces, but when they are coordinated, life feels lighter.

Healthcare deserves its own seat at the table. For many retirees, healthcare and Medicare decisions may become one of the largest and least understood forces shaping their financial future. Premiums, deductibles, prescription coverage, supplemental plans, and Medicare income-related surcharges don't just affect healthcare; they directly impact cash flow, tax planning, and long-term income sustainability.

I've seen people with solid savings plans feel blindsided by healthcare costs simply because no one helped them understand how Medicare choices intersect with income, taxes, and timing. That's why a qualified Medicare advisor is often a critical part of a coordinated retirement team—not to sell a plan, but to help ensure healthcare decisions support, rather than undermine, the rest of the retirement strategy.

A 360° VIEW MEANS SEEING EVERYTHING CLEARLY BEFORE ACTING.

A 360° view means seeing everything clearly before acting. The perspective changes the questions. Instead of "What should I do next?" they ask, "Can I trust the process to guide my decisions?" And for many, trusting the process gives their confidence room to form.

One of the biggest mistakes I see is treating life stages as separate chapters that don't overlap.

The truth is, your past decisions are funding your present and shaping your future, whether you acknowledge them or not. Your present choices have the potential to either expand your options later or quietly limit them. And your future goals only become real when today's decisions align with them.

THE 360° RETIREMENT ROADMAP[IP]

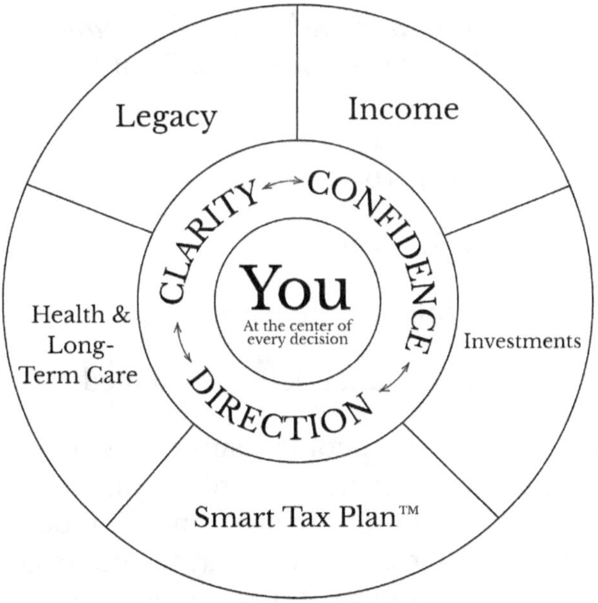

Clarity reveals the options.
Direction focuses the path.
Confidence follows — and action becomes possible.

The **360° Retirement Roadmap** connects all three at once.

It doesn't ignore where you've been.

It doesn't rush where you're going.

It helps you make thoughtful decisions in the season you're in.

This matters even more for people who are wired differently—entrepreneurs, business owners, and professionals who don't follow the traditional *work, retire, stop* pattern. For many, retirement isn't an ending; it's a redesign.

For everyone, it's a matter of understanding that confidence is built, not assumed, and readiness comes before action.

True confidence doesn't come from certainty about markets, interest rates, or life events. It is more apt to come from knowing: *I understand where I am, and I trust the process that will guide me forward.* That trust is earned when:

- the moving parts are visible
- priorities are clear
- decisions follow a thoughtful sequence
- nothing important is left unexamined

This is where some people realize they don't actually need more advice; they need coordination.

In practice, this kind of clarity and confidence often begins with a readiness check—a way to understand what's aligned, what isn't, and what deserves attention next. Not to create urgency or sell solutions, but to replace guesswork with understanding.

When we begin focusing on readiness before action, we recognize that the details matter, but first, we need to understand:

- there is a way to see the whole picture
- there is a process you can trust
- you don't have to navigate it alone

My role has never been to be the hero. I'm here to bring clarity and experienced guidance so people can make wise decisions and leave a better story behind, so no one has to travel this road alone. I've learned that the best outcomes don't come from doing more; they come from seeing clearly, choosing intentionally, and moving forward in the right order. That's what a 360° view makes possible. And once you see your life this way, direction no longer feels urgent. It feels intentional.

One Redesigned Future

When Trooper Michael Harrison came to see me at age fifty, his financial picture was strong. His early, consistent contributions and thirty-year savings habit had given him a well-funded investment plan. He had minimal debt, a growing brokerage account, and an emergency fund that rivaled those who lived in a much higher tax bracket. Still, as he prepared to step down from law enforcement, something many first responders do at age fifty, reality hit him in a different way.

"Jackie," he said, "I planned for retirement numbers and savings, not the transition away from the job itself or what's next."

That's the heart of law enforcement retirement—the identity shift is harder than the numbers. Retirement created a silence he wasn't ready for. First responders don't just lose a job; they lose a brotherhood, structure, authority, adrenaline rush, and a constant sense of being needed. Walking through that season with my husband puts me in a unique position when first responders walk into my office.

So, before Michael and I talked about income strategies, we talked about purpose and how his past and present had prepared him for his future.

- What was God calling him to now?
- Who would he be outside the uniform?
- What does service in the next season look like?
- How will he transition out of high-alert mode into rest and renewal?

Before we created his retirement roadmap, we helped map out his new identity. Since I'm a retirement planner and a wealth manager as well as a tax planner, some don't expect me to ask questions like, "If money weren't an issue, what's the one thing you would focus on?" But I believe this might be one of the most important questions we ask as we start to look forward to retirement.

I also love to use the Strategic Coach R-Factor Question®: "If we were having this discussion three years from today, and you were to look back over those three years to today, what has to have happened in your life, both personally and professionally, for you to feel happy about your progress?" This allows people to think forward and not get caught up in the dollars and cents.

A Starting Point Session helps people explore their values, verifiables (accounts and investments), and vision. These make up the foundation of a 360° Retirement Roadmap that will take you where you want to go.

With his intended purpose clearer, Michael and I set up survivor considerations for his wife and a purpose-based spending plan that included charitable giving that aligned with his faith. A 360° Retirement Roadmap better aids you in avoiding the detours that come from being lost and not having a specific destination in mind.

Evaluating Your Retirement Readiness

One question that haunts even those in higher tax brackets is: "Can I afford to retire?"

We grow accustomed to our lifestyles, and expenses don't disappear just because work does. Many people say, "I'm going to spend less in retirement," but I'm a pattern person. In many cases, whatever you're doing now, you'll want to do more, not less, when time and freedom increase.

That's why I often recommend a trial retirement. A few weeks away from work can be revealing. Some discover their interests cost very little. Others realize their dreams require more structure than they expected.

As I've said before, many people believe their IRA or 401(k) is their retirement plan. Until you understand how those assets will be converted into income and how long that income needs to last, you don't yet have a plan. You have accounts.

Some people begin this process by taking a complimentary **Risk Score Assessment**. That tool is designed to measure comfort with market volatility and helps identify whether an investment allocation aligns with emotional and financial tolerance for risk.

A Risk Score is useful, but it is only one piece of the picture.

The Financial Planning Mindset Scorecard is a professional evaluation—a structured way to help you determine whether the pieces of your financial life are coordinated well enough to support the next season of life.

As a CPA and CFP®, I've learned that readiness cannot be reduced to a single number. Two people with identical account balances—and even identical Risk Scores—can have very different levels of readiness depending on how income is structured, how exposed they are to taxes, how healthcare costs are planned for, and whether decisions are aligned with timing and purpose.

The Financial Planning Mindset Scorecard brings the Five Forces together—income, risk, liquidity, taxes, and legacy—alongside healthcare and timing. It helps identify gaps, pressure points, and blind spots **before** decisions become irreversible.

Readiness doesn't eliminate uncertainty. It replaces assumptions with clarity, urgency with order, and reaction with intention.

A Risk Score is designed to measure comfort with volatility. Retirement readiness measures preparedness for life.

This is the moment the picture comes into focus—not because every answer is known, but because you are more apt to finally see how the pieces fit together. Consider:

- What part of my life would feel lighter if I could see it from a 360° view instead of one decision at a time?
- What would change if I trusted a roadmap instead of relying on guesswork?

Cue the Confetti

A few months after retiring, Trooper Harrison sent me a picture. The text with it simply said, "Enjoying my second act," but the quiet lake, fishing pole, and sunrise breaking across the water spoke volumes. Michael's confetti moment was quieter than most, but the calm, grateful, centered photo caused me to celebrate. His peaceful weekend was the reward of his discipline, courage, and faithful planning.

First responders don't work for the money; they do it because God placed a calling on their lives. But when they look at their future from a 360° view, their orientation is restored, and they step into retirement with freedom—freedom to rest, to reconnect, to rediscover purpose—freedom to finally receive what they spent a lifetime giving.

9

My When File

The fear of death follows from the fear of life. A man who lives fully is prepared to die at any time.
—Mark Twain

Many are the plans in a person's heart, but it's the Lord's purpose that prevails.
—Proverbs 19:21 NIV

Everyone wants to leave a legacy. And while I can't control how much my clients have saved for retirement or how much they spend, I can help them get things ready for the next generation. I'm a big fan of cleaning up your own messes.

It's a big job to be someone's successor, trustee, or personal representative. This isn't a privilege or honor you're bestowing upon someone. Consider everything you own: a car, a house, toys, and personal belongings. Some people have multiple properties and accounts. And if you own a business, you've got even more issues to deal with.

Some people plan for the *what-ifs.* I've seen very few plan for *when.*

We tend to think about risk in abstract terms—market risk or economic risk. But life rarely unfolds abstractly; it happens in moments—a phone call, a hospital room, a form with questions you can't answer.

The Gift of Preparation

Preparation doesn't mean predicting the future; it's about reducing confusion when life interrupts the present. Over the years, I've seen something consistent across families of every size and circumstance: stress rarely comes from lack of money alone. It comes from missing information, unclear intentions, and unanswered questions, often when clarity matters most.

Our family learned some hard-won wisdom when two tumors ruptured in my dad's brain. Doctors had missed them. So, when it happened, we were all in shock. Thankfully, my mom, the CFO of the family, had everything in place. She quickly retrieved every paper the doctors asked for—living wills, prescriptions, medical reports—every little thing she had right at her fingertips. At the same time, I realized if something happened to her, my dad wouldn't be as efficient. Because of her organizational skills, we would have eventually found it all neat and tidy, but none of us knew exactly where she had it stashed.

This is also how we discovered the importance of a properly executed power of attorney. Dad left us before Mom had to make decisions for him, but because everything was so up-in-the-air for that month, I had a lawyer double-check my dad's power of attorney. We discovered that if something made him unconscious for an extended period, she would have had to get court-appointed guardianship over him to take money from his retirement accounts and take care of other legal actions on his behalf.

We never questioned my parents' preparations. They were both quite capable.

No matter how old your children are, they probably want to treat you with the highest respect. They won't ask whether you have all your paperwork in order. That's why, during the most difficult days, I hear people say, "I don't know where that is." "I'm not sure what they wanted." "I don't even know who to call." Those moments are heavy—not because people failed to care, but because caring wasn't organized in advance.

PREPARATION SHIFTS FROM BEING A TASK TO BECOMING AN ACT OF LOVE

It's up to you to ensure everything is in place and start the discussion with your successors so they have all the information they need. That's when preparation shifts from being a task to becoming an act of love.

Someday, someone will have to step into your life on your behalf: a spouse, a child, a sibling, a trusted friend. Preparation provides clarity. They don't have to guess or search or carry uncertainty alongside emotions. Preparation doesn't remove grief, but it can remove chaos.

The Difference Between Documents and Readiness

That's why I created the My When File. It's for "when" something happens—when you get sick, when you find yourself in a European hospital, when you are unable to make decisions, or when you pass away.

You can keep the information in a binder or in a digital file, but however you choose to organize it, the people you love need to know where to find it.

My When File focuses on documents—insurance papers, birth certificates, titles, wills, investment and banking information—all the important papers you keep in a safe place but haven't made anyone aware of their location.

But I developed My When File for a readiness that is broader than paperwork. It includes knowing where things are, how decisions connect, who should step in when something needs attention, and your final wishes. It's bigger than compliance and controlling outcomes; it's creating continuity.

My When File attempts to provide every bit of information someone would need to step in and run your life, even temporarily. This kind of preparation is rarely urgent until it suddenly is, and by then, it's often too late.

Before You Decide What to Do with Your Money

BEFORE YOU DECIDE WHAT TO DO WITH YOUR MONEY, YOU NEED A PLACE TO DECIDE "WHEN" LIFE HAPPENS.

Before you decide what to do with your money, you need a place to decide "when" life happens. My When File provides that place. In my opinion, life doesn't unfold in neat financial categories; it unfolds in seasons, events, and transitions—some expected, some not. Planning those moments requires more than projections. It requires thoughtfulness.

Preparation belongs alongside confidence and direction, not after them. When you understand where you are, when you trust the process guiding you forward, and when you orient your decisions around what truly matters, preparation becomes natural.

This is the moment preparation stops feeling like paperwork and starts feeling like care:

- If something happened tomorrow, who would need answers—and would they know where to find them?

- What would feel different if I knew the people I love wouldn't have to guess?

I encourage people to put Letters of Legacy in their My When File. My mother-in-law left each of us a letter to open after she was gone. It was a beautiful and appreciated gesture. These letters give you a final opportunity to tell your family how you feel and give them one last word of encouragement.

Other Letters of Legacy might include the stories and lifetime memories we never take time to share. As you complete something you're proud of or have an amazing experience, write it down or record it, and put it in your My When File. We might share bits and pieces of our stories throughout the years, but have you ever told the people you love the details of the dates, people, places, and events that had the most impact on your life?

Cue the Confetti

My When File exists for moments when clarity needs to show up on behalf of love. It's not about fear or worst-case thinking; it's about care, stewardship, and intention. And when you've completed this step of preparation, it's definitely a confetti moment.

I've seen families with substantial resources struggle deeply with their loved one's passing, and families with far less move forward calmly simply because the second had the clarity that comes from preparedness and the first did not.

Creating readiness for the people you love is not an obligation; it's a gift.

Part IV: Living Beyond the Money

10

From Accumulation to Distribution

The best investment you can make is in yourself.
—Warren Buffett

Prepare your work outside; get everything ready for yourself in the field, and after that build your house.
—Proverbs 24:27 ESV

For a good part of our lives, we are trained to accumulate. Earn more. Save more. Grow more. Protect more. Almost from birth, adults conditioned Baby Boomers and Gen X to think this way. Be responsible, be self-reliant, prepare for the future. Save early. Save often. Don't rely on anyone else. Delay gratification. Those lessons weren't wrong; they built discipline, resilience, and security.

We inherited the mindset from parents and grandparents who lived through extraordinarily challenging generations. They lived lives of scarcity, uncertainty, and sacrifice. From the Great Depression, war, rationing, and economic upheaval, to simply having very little, they learned lessons that they passed down quietly and consistently.

Be careful. Don't waste. You never know what could happen—a message born, not of fear, but survival.

I remember being taught to pick up a penny because every penny counts. That lesson wasn't really about money. It was about stewardship and respect, about not wasting what you've been given. For generations, those small habits mattered. But seasons change. As I write, pennies have found themselves being phased out of everyday currency. This reality quietly mirrors something deeper: the rules that once protected us don't serve us the same way forever. Wisdom doesn't cling to old, unchanging habits; it knows when and how to honor and adapt their purpose.

THE CLIMB AND DESCENT

In every life, accumulation serves a real purpose. It helps build security and create options. Accumulation gives you margin.

But eventually something shifts. The question turns from "How much can I build?" to "How do I live well with what I've built?"

That transition is an emotionally complex moment—not because people are unprepared, but because no one explains how fundamentally different this phase truly is.

For years, your financial life was about the climb. Accumulation rewarded strength, endurance, and forward momentum. Progress was visible. Accounts grew. Time felt like it was working in your favor. The focus was on adding, contributing, and building.

But the day will come when everything changes. The descent begins. You move from accumulation to distribution.

THE DAY WILL COME WHEN YOU MOVE FROM ACCUMULATION TO DISTRIBUTION.

Mountain climbers know the descent is the most dangerous part of the climb. The way you handle the terrain changes. Going down, balance matters more than speed. Precision plays a bigger role than power. Fatigue sets in. Small missteps can create outsized consequences.

Your financial life works the same way.

The skills that strengthened your accumulation phase are not the same skills that allow you to distribute well. You haven't done anything wrong; you've simply entered a new phase.

Distribution requires something more than a mere financial shift; it needs psychological change as well. When money begins moving out instead of in and balances fluctuate rather than steadily rise, it can create discomfort. As longevity becomes personal and the end feels closer, not farther away, even the best prepared begin to worry:

- Why does spending feel wrong?
- What if I take too much?
- What if I live longer than expected?

Some think these are signs of irresponsibility, but they are really signs of care. Distribution asks different questions, and it requires a new kind of confidence.

Not everyone realizes they're carrying a fear of spending until distribution begins. It isn't recklessness they're worried about; it's responsibility. They spent decades being careful, disciplined, and prepared. So when money begins moving out instead of in, hesitation feels like wisdom. But what they're really experiencing isn't irresponsibility; the fear of spending without a clear income framework.

Income Confidence Creates Added Peace of Mind

A few people erroneously believe they can find peace in their net worth; however, net worth does not create peace; income confidence does. Income confidence comes from mailbox money that you and your spouse will not outlive. At my firm, we rate its peace value according to a number of things:

- Predictability
- Sustainability
- Inflation
- Timing

Dependable income often makes decisions feel lighter. Even large portfolios can feel heavy when you can't count on a steady, scheduled income. You don't need what many would call the perfect income; I believe it just needs to be coordinated, and that happens best with the right advisor.

Many advisors are exceptionally skilled at helping people climb. They offer excellent accumulation-focused advice built around growth, contributions, and long-term horizons.

Distribution requires something different entirely.

- income engineering
- tax sequencing

- withdrawal coordination
- longevity planning
- spousal continuity
- emotional guidance during uncertainty

Planning for these requires more than advanced accumulation skills. They are different disciplines. The distribution stage isn't about replacing people. It's about recognizing that each life phase calls for a different kind of guidance. If you were mountain climbing, you wouldn't use the same gear or strategy for the descent as you did for the climb. Similarly, distribution deserves its own experience, awareness, and precision. It's vital your team understands the nuances of distribution.

Spending Is Not Failure

One of the quiet struggles I see centers around spending. People who worked hard, saved diligently, and lived responsibly sometimes feel guilty enjoying what they've built, or they worry that one wrong decision could undo decades of discipline. They hesitate to take distributions that will allow them to live comfortably.

But distribution isn't failure. It's fulfillment. Money was never meant to be an end in itself. It was meant to support life. I'm not recommending giving yourself a blank check to spend recklessly. I'm inviting you to spend intentionally without feeling bad about it.

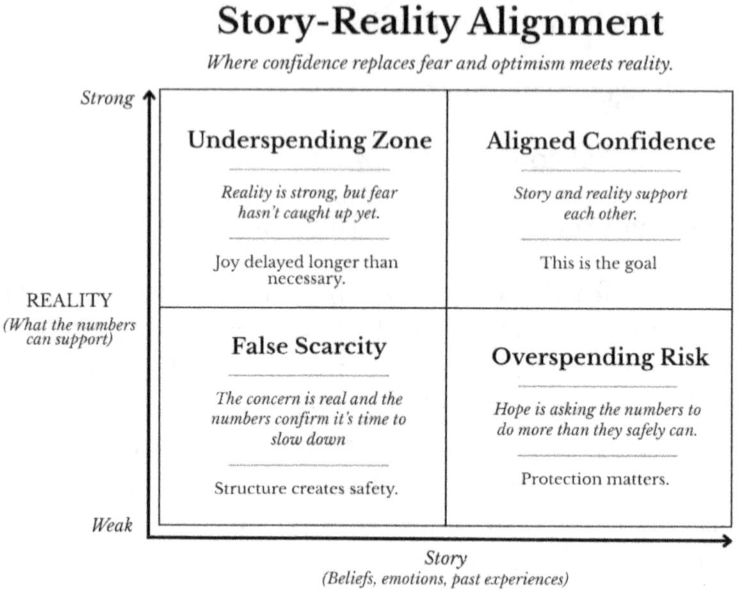

Our goal isn't permission or restriction. Our goal is alignment.

When spending aligns with values—time with family, meaningful experiences, health, generosity, freedom—it stops feeling like loss and starts feeling like purpose.

Some people need a change in mindset about their savings. In general, accumulation means preservation, and distribution means participation. From accumulation to distribution requires a shift from protecting what you've built to actively living inside it.

This is the moment you recognize distribution isn't about letting go; it's about stepping into the life you planned for—when you can confidently answer:

- What part of my life am I still holding back because spending feels like failure?
- What would change if I trusted income to support living, not just preserving?

That shift doesn't happen all at once. It comes with clarity, coordination, and experienced guidance. And when it's done well, something remarkable occurs:

- People stop watching life from the sidelines.
- They re-engage.
- They celebrate.
- They participate.

Some realize they didn't plan all those years just to feel safe. They planned to feel alive. And when the mindset shift completes, retirement stops being about money and starts being about living well beyond it.

CUE THE CONFETTI

Entering the distribution stage with anxiety and guilt is understandable after spending so many years working hard to build it. That's why you need someone who can help give you confidence when you take those first withdrawals out of your retirement investments and help you see the 360° view of your future.

You have several opportunities for confetti during this season. When you meet with an advisor who specializes in distribution, throw some confetti. After you take your first distribution, release some balloons. And when you feel that mindset shift that allows you to spend your hard-earned money guilt-free, fill the skies with confetti. You're finally beginning to fully understand life *Beyond the Money*.

11

Leaving a Legacy with Intention

The legacy of heroes is the memory of a great name and the inheritance of a great example.
—Benjamin Disraeli

Let all that you do be done in love.
—1 Corinthians 16:14 ESV

I truly want everyone to become the hero of their own financial journey. Heroes step up and take control. I know many people who have served in the military and as first responders. Though they don't think of themselves that way, we know they're heroes. The greatest heroes don't want recognition for their efforts, and they definitely don't want the things that forced them to be heroes to happen again. They are heroes because they are passionate about what they do. They want life to be better for those around them. I have a passion for helping people become the heroes of their legacy as well.

When many people hear the word legacy, they think about what they will leave behind—assets, accounts, and property.

But legacy is more than what you leave. It's what must be carried by the people you love after you're gone. Sadly, I've seen families inherit confusion right along with their money. But I've also seen families inherit clarity, confidence, and added peace of mind, even when the size of the estate was small.

Everyone leaves a legacy. Why shouldn't you be intentional about it?

Legacy Begins Long Before the End

Legacy is not something you create at the finish line; I believe it's shaped over time through conversation, organization, and the decisions you make while you're still here to explain. That's why it's an essential part of your One Financial Life.

The people who come behind you want to honor you. Whether it's after you're gone or as they walk with you through a serious illness, they respect you and want to carry out your wishes. For many, you're already their hero because of the impact you've made in their lives. When you clean up your mess before you go, you can be confident that you're leaving a hero's legacy.

Thoughtful legacy planning doesn't begin with documents. It begins with awareness:

- What matters to you?
- Who are you trying to protect?
- What would make things easier for the people you love?
- What do you want remembered—and what do you want avoided?

The questions that make the most difference are not financial questions. They are stewardship questions.

What You Leave and What You Prevent

There is one aspect of legacy stewardship some may overlook. It's easy to focus on making sure things go where we want them to go. Few even think about making sure they do not go where they don't want them to go.

I've seen life insurance paid to an ex-spouse because no one updated the beneficiary forms. I've seen retirement accounts with no beneficiaries listed at all, forcing them into probate. I've seen carefully written estate plans completely overridden by outdated account titles and neglected paperwork.

I wish I could say these situations are rare, but they're more common than anyone would like to admit. It's not that people don't care, but no one explained how easily misalignment happens.

LEGACY REQUIRES COORDINATION

To me, legacy requires coordination. Beneficiaries, account titles, estate documents, and state laws all have to work together. When they don't, it leaves families with confusion, delay, unnecessary expense, and sometimes conflict that never needed to exist.

Clarity Is an Act of Love

One of the greatest gifts you can give the people you love is clarity. Clear instructions. Clear organization. Clear intentions. You don't have to decide everything today, but when you do, those decisions should be documented, updated often, and accessible.

Clarity says, "I cared enough to think this through so you wouldn't have to carry it alone."

Legacy planning by design is more than just what happens after you're gone. It's also about bringing clarity if something happens to interrupt your ability to speak or act for yourself.

I believe every person over the age of eighteen should have a properly prepared and executed durable power of attorney under the laws of their state of residency. These documents allow someone you trust to act on your behalf if you are unable to do so yourself. Requirements regarding notaries and witnesses vary by state. Some are best prepared with the guidance of an attorney. What matters most is that they are valid where you live and accessible when needed.

In addition to a durable power of attorney, it's important to have a healthcare advocate or healthcare power of attorney (called different things per state), along with a living will that clearly expresses their wishes. A last will and testament remains foundational, and for some families, a revocable trust may be appropriate depending on assets, family dynamics, and goals.

Preparing these documents does not mean you are anticipating the worst. They mean you are preparing for when, not if, life happens, because it will. They allow decisions to be made with dignity instead of delay, and with clarity instead of conflict.

Two things in life are certain: death and taxes. Thoughtful planning doesn't remove those realities, but it can dramatically reduce confusion, cost, and burden for the people you love.

This, too, is stewardship.

Legacy Is Values, Not Just Assets

We pass down so much more than money. Our loved ones inherit our habits, our beliefs, our priorities, and our examples. Intentional legacy planning can become one of the values you pass down. When you focus on giving this gift to your loved ones, the planning becomes less about control and more about care.

Legacy isn't about preserving everything exactly as it was. Some of the rules that protected us won't always serve the next generation in the same way. Preparing your legacy is about passing on what matters most—wisdom, discernment, and values—while allowing the application to evolve.

A Better Story to Leave Behind

My role has never been to be the hero of someone else's story. I want to bring clarity and experienced guidance so people can make wise decisions and leave a better story behind—a story told in more than mere dollars. It's a story told in ease of transition, in understanding and added peace of mind, and in families who are spared confusion at an already difficult moment.

When we approach legacy this way, it stops feeling heavy and begins feeling meaningful because people understand that what they are really leaving behind is not just what they owned, but how well they cared.

This is the moment legacy stops feeling like something you leave someday and starts feeling like something you live every day.

- What kind of clarity would I want the people I love to inherit from me?
- What would it look like to leave fewer questions and more peace behind?

Cue the Confetti

We don't want you to be like one of those people who wait until the hurricane hits to gather the flashlights and water bottles. Those of us who live near the Gulf know that's not a prudent idea. The same principle applies to planning for your retirement or the storms of life. You want the power to make decisions based on good days and fair weather, rather than torrential rains.

Campbell & Company believes legacy planning allows you to take care of the people you love by preparing thoughtfully while you still can. Every time you put another piece of paper or a digital document in your My When File, it's time for a celebration. Each letter you write, each memory you share, every item you cross off your bucket list is a confetti moment.

12

Confetti Moments

He has achieved success who has lived well, laughed often, and loved much.
—Bessie Anderson Stanley

One generation shall commend your works to another, and shall declare your mighty acts.
—Psalm 145:4 ESV

For many years, life feels like preparation. We prepare for work, prepare for family, prepare for retirement, prepare for "someday." We tell ourselves we'll slow down later; we'll celebrate when we have more time; we'll enjoy life when things are clearer, safer, and more certain.

But experience has taught me a couple of things:

Someday is built out of moments.

And moments don't wait.

Confetti moments are rarely loud or planned far in advance. They often arrive right after the fear of spending loosens its grip, and intention replaces guilt. And many times they are quiet, unexpected, fleeting. Sadly, when we're not paying attention, they pass without being fully lived.

NOT ABOUT PERFECTION

Planning well isn't meant to delay joy; it's meant to make room for it. Confetti moments aren't about perfect timing, perfect health, or perfect circumstances. They're about presence: a shared meal, a meaningful trip, a spontaneous "yes," a quiet conversation, or a memory that stays with you long after the moment ends.

PREPARING YOUR LEGACY GOES BEYOND THE MONEY

Money matters. It always has. But preparing your legacy goes beyond the money. At my firm, it's about Clarity, Direction, and Confidence. I want to help you understand where you are, to trust the process that will guide you forward, and move into the next season of life without fear. You don't need everything to be solved to celebrate, but when the picture is finally clear enough to take the next step, it's time for a confetti moment. Confetti moments happen when the weight of what-if loosens just enough for gratitude to step in. They don't have to be extravagant; they just have to be noticed.

This is the moment we want you to realize you don't have to wait for everything to be finished before you celebrate.

- What moment in my life right now deserves more attention than I've been giving it?

- What would change if I let gratitude lead instead of postponing joy?

A Life Lived on Purpose Feels Different

A coordinated financial life creates the opportunity for a life shift. It doesn't need to be perfect. Your One Financial Life simply needs to be lived intentionally with Clarity, Direction, and Confidence. How would it feel to stop second-guessing every decision or carrying everything alone?

When you become intentional with your plan, confetti moments show up more often. It's not that life gets easier, but because you're finally present enough to receive them. It's as if you put legs on your legacy.

In my life, putting legs on my legacy means having a 100 Day Succession Plan[IP] in place for my partners and having My When File up to date. I don't intend to retire anytime soon, but the plan means my team and my family know what to expect when I decide I'm ready to transition into my next phase of life.

These intentional steps made my hero journey a little more real.

Putting legs on your legacy means grabbing your bucket list and doing something with it. If you've done a great job of saving during your working years, it's time to give yourself permission to spend so you can do some of those things you've been dreaming of.

It also means being intentional with everything you've built and fought for. It's implementing the plan you've created for your investment of blood, sweat, and tears. Even if you plan to work for twenty more years, completing your My When File will give you added peace of mind and make you a hero to your spouse, children, grandchildren, and friends.

Become the Hero of Your Story

You might be at the end of this book, but you've reached the beginning of the conversation. It's a conversation that starts when you notice things that feel heavy or unfinished. It's a story you write when you pay attention to what brings peace and what quietly drains it. From there, the path forward becomes surprisingly clear, not perfect, but making progress. And thoughtful progress creates space for life to be lived, not just managed.

I'm working on Confetti Notes[IP] right now. Every time I think of someone who influenced my past, I want to reach out with a note or a call and intentionally thank them for what they gave me. Thank you for the advice. Thank you for the lessons. Thank you for the encouragement or the example. Thank you for being part of a special day in my life. Showing gratitude while you and the person who impacted your life are still alive can be a powerful confetti moment for both of you.

Gratitude left unspoken is a gift never fully given.

I want to help you embrace intentionality long before you need to. Financial freedom is marked by wisdom. It's a story marked by care. A life marked by gratitude. A hero's journey marked by moments worth celebrating.

As you move forward on your path, I hope you carry this with you:

Plan well.

Live fully.

And when confetti moments arrive, big or small, don't rush past them. They are the reason you plan in the first place.

Epilogue

When we think about the mile markers of our life, it's easy to focus on the landslides and roadblocks. But even your worst year has confetti moments if you are willing to look for them. Recently, someone asked me the Michael Hyatt question, "What needs to happen to make this the best year ever?"

My mind immediately went to a trip my husband and I took to Wyoming, a trip I'll never forget. We got up early to a beautiful snow globe kind of day. Perfect weather for a magical dog sledding adventure. The newly fallen snow made the excursion perfect.

The next evening, we were in the emergency room. My husband experienced heart issues due to altitude challenges. What a drastic difference a few hours can make. "It was the best of times. It was the worst of times." And somehow, both were true at once. Yet the trip was still confetti-worthy.

The year my dad died clarified the importance of family and an appreciation for the way we all pulled together. It was a horrible thing, yet the beauty of everyone surrounding us with support turned into a confetti moment.

Don't let the detours keep you from celebrating the milestones of each season. Every unexpected route offers adventure and sights we might not otherwise get to see. Watch carefully for the wonderful, and keep the confetti close!

Your legacy is more than how much you leave in a bank account. So many other things outweigh the dollars. The amount of time you spend with your family and friends and the way you live out your faith are two things that shape your legacy.

In my life, I sometimes struggle between being with my mom, who lives five hours away, spending time with my children and grandchildren, and doing this work I love. When I'm in my childhood home, I can't be with my grandchildren. When I'm here, I miss my mother. But I've learned to celebrate my awareness and intention rather than focusing on the struggle. I want to make an impact on their lives as well as the lives of my family and friends.

I've discovered faith brings steadiness, hope, and peace, especially in seasons marked by stress or uncertainty. Whatever your belief system, embrace it and let it guide the way you live. My Christian faith emphasizes love, joy, peace, and patience. It encourages me to be still and trust in something bigger than myself.

When we celebrate the things money can't buy, we build a legacy that will make the next generation stronger, and we enjoy a future that goes *Beyond the Money*.

Resources

The concepts shared in this book are general in nature and may not apply to every individual or situation. Professional guidance is essential when making financial, tax, legal, or investment decisions.

My When File™ Checklist

Essential	What It Covers	Why It Matters
Health & Medical Decisions	Directives, POA, doctors, meds, Medicare, LTC	Guides medical decisions with clarity and authority.
Legal & Estate Documents	Will, trust, POA, guardianship, instructions	Prevents conflict and court intervention.
Finances & Beneficiaries	Accounts, insurance, income sources, beneficiaries	Ensures assets flow smoothly to intended recipients.
Household & Property Details	Home, utilities, insurance, maintenance, titles	Keeps daily life functional during a crisis.
Personal Notes & Final Wishes	Letters, scripture, funeral wishes, values	Offers comfort, meaning, and legacy.

RETIREMENT OPERATING SYSTEM BY DECADE

Decade	*Focus*	*Theme*
20s: Building the Base	Foundations	Habits matter more than protection
30s: Build Momentum	Direction & Protection	Direction beats speed
40s: Build Alignment	Optimization	Alignment over accumulation
50s: Build Opportunity	Preparation	Options create confidence
60s: Build the Retirement Paycheck	Coordination	Coordination replaces accumulation
70s: Build Tax Efficiency and Legacy	Stewardship	Control Taxes; don't let them control you
80s & Beyond: Build Simplicity	Ease & Legacy	A well-organized life is a gift

Financial Planning Mindset Scorecard

CAMPBELL & COMPANY

Choose the number that corresponds your level of preparedness

	1 2 3	4 5 6	7 8 9	10 11 12	13 14 15	Score
Retirement Preparedness	Retirement is a very long way off and I haven't given it much thought.	I put the minimum in my 401k account every month.	I have a clear retirement vision and know how much income I'll need.	I'm confident I have enough to support my retirement, with multiple income streams in place.	I have more than I need and am exploring a philanthropic foundation.	
Income & Expenses	I still rely on credit cards and find it hard to get ahead.	I have some savings and spend less than I earn each month.	I have six months of emergency savings and contribute to my 401(k).	I have built savings, reduced debt, and maximize my 401(k) contributions.	I have ample cash reserves, excess income, and a sizable investment portfolio.	
Investments	I don't have investments and feel uncertain about the stock market.	I have a 401(k) and inherited investments but need a better understanding of my accounts.	I contribute enough to my 401(k) to receive my employer match and use a target date fund.	I have a diversified retirement portfolio aligned with my risk tolerance.	I have multiple assets and am seeking safe solutions for surplus cash and income.	
Health/Long Term Care	I don't have insurance and don't really need it, knock on wood	I have insurance at work.	I have health coverage but no long-term care insurance.	I have full health and long-term care coverage to protect our assets.	I have Medicare, insurance protection, and long-term care strategies.	
Legal	I don't trust lawyers	I don't care what happens when I die	My intentions are clear, but my estate plan is not complete.	I have a will and updated beneficiary designations on my accounts.	I have a will, trust, and beneficiaries aligned with my legacy goals.	
Taxes	I hate taxes, but death and taxes are unavoidable.	I use free tax software but need help planning for taxes.	My uncle does my taxes.	I work with a CPA who helps me minimize my tax burden.	My advisor is a CPA who provides ongoing investment and tax planning.	

You will find additional resources available at BeyondTheMoneyBook.com:

Endnotes

1. Rogers, Kenny, and Parton, Dolly. *Warner Music Nashville.* "Kenny Rogers-You Can't Make Old Friends (duet with Dolly Parton) [Official Video]. November 27, 2013. https://www.youtube.com/watch?v=chBNBzE35EI.

2. *Strategic Coach.* "The Gap and the Gain." Accessed November 7, 2025. https://gapandgainbook.com/.

Acknowledgments

Teach us to number our days,
that we may gain a heart of wisdom.
—Psalm 90:12

I chose this verse because it reflects the heart behind this book: to live intentionally, steward our time with purpose, and recognize that wisdom is something we gain through the seasons of our life—not at the finish line, but along the journey itself.

For many years, I believed inner peace was something I had to reach, a place somewhere beyond the next accomplishment or milestone. But with time, faith, and the people God has placed in my life, I've learned that peace isn't a destination at all. It's a companion we grow into, shaped by grace, experience, and the wisdom collected along the way.

This book is part of that unfolding.

I was blessed with **extraordinary grandparents**, each leaving a meaningful and lasting imprint on my life. Their faith, strength, steady presence, and deeply rooted values shaped the person I am today. Alongside them, my parents, aunts, and uncles surrounded me with encouragement, love, stability, and a strong sense of tradition. Their influence is woven into every page of this book.

To **my mom, Linda, and my dad, Jack**, thank you for the values you instilled, the work ethic you modeled, and the unwavering support you've given me through every chapter of my life. You taught me what commitment, faith, and integrity truly look like.

To **Scott**, my husband and high school sweetheart, a retired Florida State Trooper and lifelong protector. Thank you for your service to our community, your wisdom, and the quiet strength with which you've protected our family. Building a life and legacy with you has been one of my greatest blessings.

To my children, **Jacob and Brooke,**

Jacob, your creativity and free spirit have filled my life with possibility and perspective.

Brooke, your grounded steadiness and the truth that you have raised me in many ways have given me strength. The humor we share remains one of life's greatest gifts.

To **Chuck**, my son-in-law, thank you for the calm, grounded presence you bring to our family and for being such a devoted father. Your steadiness matters more than you know.

To my granddaughters, **Stevie and Drew,** may you grow with courage, kindness, and wisdom. May you learn to honor your time, trust your instincts, and build lives that feel both meaningful and true. And may you always remember to celebrate the confetti moments—the small joys, quiet wins, and meaningful milestones that make life rich and worth savoring. My hope is that the world you inherit is shaped by people who choose integrity, stewardship, and care, and that you always know how deeply you are loved.

To **Brooke and Scott,** thank you for standing beside me not only as family, but as contributors to the strength and future of Campbell & Company. You represent continuity, shared vision, and a deep commitment to doing the right thing.

To **Monica Haberlin Wahl,** thank you for more than twenty-five years of unwavering dedication to Campbell & Company. Your leadership, loyalty, and gift for bringing order and harmony have made you the steady heartbeat of our firm. As our Integrator, you help turn vision into reality every day.

To **Jim Wilhelm,** thank you for the wisdom, steadiness, and integrity you bring to every decision and every season. Your leadership continues to strengthen our firm from the inside out.

To **Randy Kardas,** thank you for your innovation, dedication, and ability to turn ideas into reality. Your passion for building thoughtful solutions has become essential to our growth.

To the entire **Campbell & Company team, past and present,** thank you for your heart, dedication, and belief in our mission. Together, you create an experience rooted in clarity, integrity, and genuine care for the families we serve.

To **Ron Eastman,** mentor, truth-teller, and steady encourager, thank you for your patience, wisdom, and for seeing more in me than I sometimes saw in myself.

To **Mike Macho,** thank you for your belief in my being uniquely myself and for helping me find my voice.

To **Mark Owens,** thank you for your professionalism, quick wit, and steady presence as a cohost and friend. You elevate every conversation.

To **Kim Skouras,** thank you for your insight, encouragement, and thoughtful challenge. Your influence has left a lasting mark.

To my niece, **Madison Yates**—thank you for sharing your talent and capturing the photography that helps bring *Beyond the Money* to life.

To **Grace King**, my Content & Strategy Specialist—thank you for your never-ending care, follow-through, and passion in helping me bring *Beyond the Money* to life and reach this very special birthday goal.

To **Dan Sullivan**, founder of Strategic Coach, and to **the Strategic Coach community, including my guides Mary Miller, Chad Johnson, and Stephanie Song,** thank you for the thinking, frameworks, and steady coaching that reshaped how I understand time, leadership, and long-term growth. Your questions, perspective, and guidance helped me translate ideas into action, growth into clarity, and vision into decisions that endure.

To the **mentors, CPAs, financial advisors, business professionals, and trusted guides** who shaped me from the earliest days of my career, thank you for your generosity, your standards, and your willingness to teach. You modeled what it means to lead with integrity, serve with humility, and care deeply about the people behind the numbers. My hope is that this work reflects your influence and continues the shared calling of guiding others with wisdom, clarity, and purpose.

To **the Impact Partnership team,** thank you for your creativity, support, and belief in this message. Your partnership helped shape both the voice and the reach of this book.

To the **Blue Line family**, your courage, sacrifice, and quiet commitment have shaped my life and perspective more than words can express. You will always have a place in my heart and in this work.

To **our clients, client families, and entrepreneurs,** thank you for trusting us with your stories, your questions, your fears, and your futures. You are the reason this work matters.

And finally, to **you, the reader,** thank you for inviting me into your story. My hope is that these pages offer Clarity, Direction, and Confidence and remind you that it's not too late to make wise decisions, and it's not wrong to want a life that feels both secure and meaningful.

ABOUT THE AUTHOR

Jackie Campbell has built her career in the insurance and tax preparation industries, serving as a trusted advisor to families and businesses. She has held a Series 65 license since 2014, further expanding her ability to guide clients in financial matters. She enjoys guiding people through the pivotal financial crossroads of life—the milestones, the birthdays, and the "what's next" decisions that define their futures. A financial advisor, entrepreneur, author, and creator of patent-pending proprietary financial technology, she understands firsthand that retirement looks different for everyone, especially for entrepreneurs, high-achieving professionals, and families navigating transition. Jackie's mission is to help create 10,000 heroes of their own financial story, guiding people with clarity, confidence, and direction while encouraging them to celebrate the "confetti moments" that make the journey meaningful.

As host of the popular podcasts *Beyond the Money* and *Beyond the BADGE*, Jackie speaks directly to these audiences, offering both wisdom and encouragement. Whether it's a business owner considering succession, a professional hitting a milestone birthday, or a widow facing life's next chapter, Jackie brings both practical strategies and heartfelt guidance. Her approach blends time-tested financial wisdom with the personal side of transition, reminding readers that planning is not about restriction, but about creating the space to fully live.

CONNECT WITH JACKIE

Join the ongoing conversation about money, meaning, leadership, and life—beyond the numbers.

Follow along for insights, stories, and real-world perspectives as you navigate what's next.

MyCampbellAndCo.com

www.ingramcontent.com/pod-product-compliance
Lightning Source LLC
LaVergne TN
LVHW010730061126
851857LV00014B/1414
* 9 7 8 1 6 3 6 8 0 5 7 1 9 *